Affectionately
Franklin Taylor Nevius
Sewickley
December 1929

University of Pittsburgh Bradford

The T. Edward and
Tullah Hanley Library

This Item Presented By

Richard Lutz

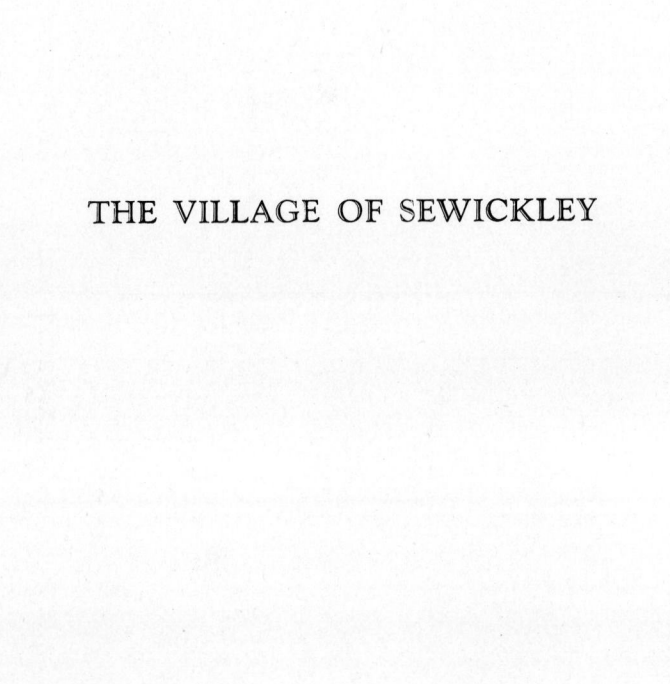

THE VILLAGE OF SEWICKLEY

THE SHIELDS HOUSE, ONCE SEWICKLEY BOTTOM POST OFFICE

THE
VILLAGE OF SEWICKLEY

BY

FRANKLIN TAYLOR NEVIN

WITH AN INTRODUCTION BY
ALEXANDER C. ROBINSON
PRESIDENT OF PEOPLES-PITTSBURGH TRUST COMPANY
PITTSBURGH - PENNSYLVANIA

END-PAPERS DESIGNED BY
AUDLEY DEAN NICOLS
SEWICKLEY, PENNSYLVANIA - EL PASO, TEXAS

PUBLISHED BY
THE SEWICKLEY PRINTING-SHOP
SEWICKLEY - PENNSYLVANIA
1929

Copyright, 1929, by
THE SEWICKLEY PRINTING-SHOP, Inc.

INTRODUCTION

SEWICKLEY has always had an individual character of its own, but the powerful modern forces working for standardization of life, thought, and customs throughout the country, such as the multiplication in the means of transport and increase in the speed of travel, tend rapidly to destroy this self-contained and interesting quality. To cite but one example, the old stores with the personalities of their proprietors, are being replaced by the impersonal and foreign owned chain stores. This is in the line of present economic development, but it makes it the more important that the records of the old, and in many respects, unique community should be put in permanent form while it is still possible to do so.

Topographically the widening of the level ground at this point on the river naturally early attracted settlers, and the place was just the right distance from Pittsburgh for the flat boats floating down or being laboriously poled up the river to be stopped for a noonday meal or for a night at a local tavern. The same thing was true of the stage coaches and wagons driving along the Beaver Post Road. So Sewickley began and its semi-isolation combined with the strong characters of its early settlers made it a distinctive and self reliant community in its civic and cultural life. It developed its own resources, furnished its own amusements and recreations. Growing slowly and free from the influences of large industries, there was more of personal acquaintance and community of interest uninfluenced by distinctions of wealth or social position. This remained true long after the coming of the railroad turned its male population so largely into daily commuters to Pittsburgh for business, and the city shops and amusements became more available.

The town, nevertheless, was never provincial in its attitude and outlook. It took a wide and intelligent interest in the affairs of the country and of the whole world, and felt itself part of them, while preserving its own integrity and individuality.

Sewickley (and this of course includes the immediately adjoining boroughs, for the differences are only those of municipal divisions) has always held the affection and justified pride of its residents. Those who have read in *The Herald* Mr. Nevin's descriptions of the Sewickley which was, but is now passing, will rejoice that they have been gathered into permanent form, and those to whom they now come as new will equally find them delightful.

No one is better qualified than Mr. Nevin for this work. Coming of a family which had so large a part in forming the life and development of the Valley he is fully fitted by his own tastes, education, ability, and interest to be its historian and biographer.

The history of the Sewickley Valley, the reminiscences of the individual and forceful men and women who lived in it, are well worth preserving, and Mr. Nevin has done this well. Those who have tender associations with the Valley, its hills and its streams, its homes and its activities, are under deep obligation to Mr. Nevin. That this book has to him been a labor of love but adds to its value, and has increased his understanding and sympathetic handling of the varied material.

ALEXANDER C. ROBINSON.

FOREWORD

The papers which make up this volume, with a few exceptions, appeared originally in the *Sewickley Herald* through whose courtesy they are here republished. Acknowledgment is due to the trustees of the Presbyterian Church of Sewickley for permission to reprint the *Historical Sketch* which was included in the copyrighted volume issued in 1914 on the occasion of that church's seventy-fifth anniversary celebration. In the preparation of that paper valuable manuscripts in the possession of Mr. Gilbert A. Hays were consulted as were the following authorities: *Presbyterianism in the Sewickley Valley* by Rev. James Allison, 1876; *The Fiftieth Anniversary Exercises of the Presbyterian Church,* Sewickley, Pa., 1888; *The Olden Time in Sewickley* by John Way, Jr.; *Lights and Shadows of Sewickley Life* by Agnes L. Ellis, 1891; *The Qui Vive,* Sewickley, 1885; and *Settlements and Land Titles of Northwestern Pennsylvania,* by Judge Agnew of Beaver, Pa. Mr. Harrison D. Mason's charming volume of *Memories* furnished the description of Syd Sawyer and the country store at Stoops Ferry, and thanks are due to Mrs. Francis M. Hutchinson and to descendants of William Stoops and Jacob Lashell for the loan of family portraits. An especially valuable source of information was the marvelously clear memory for facts and dates which Captain John C. Anderson drew upon in conversations about the old days.

Written at various times and without continuity the several papers have been here arranged with some sequence, some relation to the periods to which they refer. Certain references here and there to matters contemporaneous with the first appearance of the articles have been allowed to remain in the present text, although those references are now out of date.

In presuming to embody these random notes and memories in book form the thought has been to preserve something of the village atmosphere, something of the simplicity that marked our lives and recreations in a day now fast receding into the once-upon-a-time. It is hoped that older readers may have pleasant memories revived and that an occasional younger one may catch a glimpse of the Village of Sewickley as it was in a quieter and less strenuous age.

FRANKLIN TAYLOR NEVIN.

Sewickley, Pa., September, 1929.

FRANKLIN TAYLOR NEVIN

CONTENTS

Sewickley: A Historical Sketch	11
Addy Beer's Grove	53
Old Sewickley Taverns	59
Early Sewickley	67
Sewickley Rivermen	77
Sewickley Railroad Men	85
The Passing of Two Landmarks	95
A Ferry Tale	101
Harbaugh's Pond	111
On the Way to School	117
The Friendly River	123
The Belva Dears	131
McDonald's Grove	137
The Sewickley Athletic Association	143
When Bicycling was a Sport	151
Rock Spring and the Camel Back	161
When Coxey Came	167
Sewickley's Colored Pioneers	175
Pittsburgh to Bedford by Carriage	193
Loretto and Aleppo	203
Pittsburgh in 1815	211

SEWICKLEY: A HISTORICAL SKETCH

SEWICKLEY

A HISTORICAL SKETCH

IN the settlement of western Pennsylvania, that region lying to the north and west of the Ohio and Allegheny rivers was considerably later in its development than the land to the south. A number of causes combined to bring this about. The southern territory, particularly that along the Monongahela River, was more readily accessible to settlers coming from the east by way of the Short Route, as it was called, which left the Potomac valley at Wills Creek (Cumberland, Md.) and struck directly across to Redstone (Brownsville), on the Monongahela, a popular highway of trade and migration. Powerful influences deterring settlers from crossing into the country north of the Ohio were the hostile Indians and the uncertainty of land titles due to the conflicting claims to that territory which were strongly maintained by the Virginia and Pennsylvania colonies. Penn's grant ran five degrees of longitude west from the Delaware River, but just how far that was no one knew. Virginia boldly claimed everything to the north and west, and created two counties, Frederick and Augusta, which extended indefinitely, covering what is now some fifty or sixty counties and four or five states. She only relinquished her claim in 1779, when the Pennsylvania and Virginia boundaries were settled by a commission which extended Mason and Dixon's line to a point five degrees west of the Delaware, and, a few years later, ran a line directly north from that point to form the western boundary of Pennsylvania. This disputed territory was not so well adapted to farming as was that to the south, and this was yet another cause of its isolation. It had no army roads, no considerable streams; it was traversed by only a few Indian trails. In fact, after the expulsion of the French, it was long left to the Indians, its original owners.

When Colonel Bouquet, in 1764, conducted his expedition against the Indians in "Muskingum County," as the country to the far west was called, he followed a course through the lowlands of what is now the North Side of Pittsburgh, to the "Narrows" and thence proceeded along the Ohio River beach to Beaver Creek. The regular line of communication between Fort Pitt and Fort McIntosh (Beaver) was a longer route by a military road, on the south side of the river, which passed near Sharon church, now Carnot post-office.

On October 23, 1784, the Indians' title to the land north of the river was extinguished by a deed to the state from the Six Nations, in consideration of the sum of $5,000. This was effected by a treaty made at Fort Stanwix, in New York state. In the following year, 1785, by another treaty, made at Fort McIntosh, the interests of the Delawares and Wyandots were purchased for $3,000, additional. These sub-tribes were, in effect, terre-tenants under the more powerful Iroquois, who looked upon them as a conquered and subservient race.

While yet a colony, Pennsylvania, in 1771, had erected the county of Bedford, embracing all of its southwestern territory. In 1773 Westmoreland County was carved out of this unwieldy subdivision. In 1781 all of the land south and west of the Monongahela and Ohio was made into Washington County, the first county created after the colony had become a state, and in 1788 Allegheny County, reaching clear to Lake Erie, was in turn cut out of Westmoreland.

While Allegheny County was still a part of Westmoreland, the so-called "New Purchase" was divided into two great sections by a due east-and-west line running from Mogulbughtiton (Mahoning) Creek, on the Allegheny River, above Kittanning, to the western border of the state. The land south of this line was appropriated to the redemption of the depreciation certificates which had been given to the officers and soldiers of the Pennsylvania line in payment for their services in the War of the Revolution. These allotments were called "Depreciation Lands" and Sewickley is of course included therein. The land north of the line was known as "Donation

Land," and was given to officers and soldiers according to their rank and service. The Depreciation Lands were laid out under the direction of the Surveyor General in lots of not less than 250 nor more than 350 acres each and were put on sale in numerical order, under certain restrictions, to be paid for in gold, silver, or in depreciation certificates. Major Daniel Leet and Nathaniel Breading surveyed those sections within which Sewickley lies, the division between their respective districts being a line which ran due north from the Ohio River to the above described east-and-west line, a distance of about thirty miles. A part of the lower end of this line is still marked by what remains of Division Street, in the borough.

Popular tradition has it that the name Sewickley is derived from an Indian word meaning "sweet water," allusion being made to the sugar maples called *Seweekly* trees, which abounded in this and other localities so named. Charles A. Hanna, in his exhaustive study of the early history of this region, *The Wilderness Trail* (published in 1911), says (vol. i, page 298): "The name of the Asswikales Indians who came from South Carolina has been preserved to the present day under the form of Sewickley, a name now applied to two creeks, forty miles apart, one on the east and the other on the west side of Pittsburgh." Elsewhere he gives the following variants of the tribal name, some of which result from differences in the native dialects: Assekales, Asswekalaes, Shaweygilas, and Shaweygiras. The oldest form, he says, appears to have been Sawakola or Sawokli, derived from two Indian words *sawi*, raccoon, and *ukli* town. The New York *Evening Post,* in its review of Mr. Hanna's book, goes on to say: "The Assiwikalas, from whom Sewickley, Pa., takes its name, were the Hathiwikala, or Absentee Shawnee, one of the five (not four) original sub-tribes of the Shawnee, but always in history keeping somewhat aloof from the others. It is quite possible that they were the Sawokli, or Souikila, incorporated with the Creeks."

As a sidelight upon the unsettled question of the name's derivation it is worthy of note that in Marion County, West

Virginia, there is a vein of coal that is shown on old title abstracts as the "Mapletown or Sewickley" vein and the two names appear to be used interchangeably, which is some evidence of a tradition current there as with us that Sewickley took its name from the *seweekly* or maple trees.

Be the derivation of the name as it may, the earliest mention of Sewickley as the name of a locality seems to have been in the form "Sewichly Old Town," in a grant from the Six Nations to George Croghan, dated 1749. This probably stood on the Youghiogheny River at the mouth of the Big Sewickley Creek in Westmoreland County, though there is some authority for supposing it to have been located on the Allegheny River near the present site of Tarentum.

In an interesting letter, now in the possession of Mr. Gilbert A. Hays, which is dated at Pittsburgh, 31st December 1767, and written by one John Campbell, an Indian trader, reference is made for the first time, so far as is now known, to the Sewickley lying on the north bank of the Ohio River. He says: "Four Men that I sent off in a Cannoe and who had gone but a short Distance below the Point had nearly been overset, and with great Difficulty returned without daring to attempt the Recovery of the Batteau. She was seen passing the Sewicly Bottom (a Place about 12 or 14 miles off,) that Night and was sound."

The locality is named again as early as the year 1779, when the Delaware Indians, in gratitude for his treatment of them, offered to Colonel George Morgan, the first Indian agent at Fort Pitt, as a free gift, a strip of land extending roughly from what is now Haysville to Legionville and back to the tops of the highest hills, including the Sewickley Bottom, a tract possibly six miles long by three wide. This gift Colonel Morgan declined to accept in return for "merely doing his duty," as he expressed it.

To return to the allotments of land in this locality: Major Daniel Leet's survey comprised nine lots in District No. 2, which began at the present Division Street and extended to and included Leetsdale. He took by patent lots 6, 7, 8, and 9, called respectively Lincoln, Locust Bottom, Sugar Bottom, and Leetsburg. Later he purchased lots 3, 4, and 5, named Newburg, Norwich, and Newington. Lot No. 1, called Loretto, a 250-acre tract which includes the western half of the borough, was purchased at the government sale at the Old Coffee House, Philadelphia, by Levi Hollingsworth who, before receiving the patent, transferred it to Mark Wilcox, who conveyed it to Jonathan Leet, by whom it was in turn sold in 1798 to Henry Ulery, a German sea-captain, and the first white settler on the land now Sewickley. This sale is recorded in the Recorder's office of Allegheny County, in Deed Book, vol. 8, at page 111. Lot No. 2, known as Way's Desire, consisted of 200 acres and lay next to Loretto, extending from the present western limits of the borough and including the eastern portion of the present Edgeworth borough. It was bought in 1785 by Caleb Way of Chester County, ancestor of the Ways who still hold the greater portion of it. John Way, son of Caleb, occupied the tract in 1797, and lived in a log house which stood near the present site of the Sewickley electric light plant, at Quaker Valley. In 1810 he built on the Beaver Road the first brick house between Pittsburgh and Beaver, which is now occupied by his descendant, Judge William A. Way.

Adjoining Loretto on the east, in Breading's District, was the tract called Aleppo, containing 234 acres, 91 perches. This was bought from the state by Henry Pratt in 1786. He sold it to Jonathan Leet, by whom it was conveyed to one John Vail, and by him in turn to Thomas Beer, the settler, in 1802. (Deed Book, vol. 11, page 57.) The eastern limit of this farm was near the present Glen Osborne station. Mr. Beer built the frame house which is still standing on the river bank beside the McMillen lumber-yard, at Glen Osborne station, and there made his home. Henry Ulery, who had bought Loretto, built for himself a log house near where the Park Place Hotel now stands. In 1810 he sold his farm to Thomas Hoey, the grandfather of Mrs. Judge White and Mrs. William Harbaugh. When we say *farm,* it must not be understood that it was at that time under cultivation. Mrs. Harbaugh used to tell how, as a child, when accompanying her father, the Rev. Charles Thorn, to the "village," she would cling tightly to his hand, when entering the dense chestnut woods which began at about where the railroad now is. The dark woods were full of terrors for her childish imagination.

On the line dividing the Ulery and Beer lands an acre was set apart by the two owners as a burying-ground, during the plague years 1809-10. This lay just east of the present Gilmore residence, 653 Bank Street. The road leading to this spot was long known as Graveyard Lane, now Division Street. Mr. Hoey subsequently built a stone house near the site of Ulery's log cabin, and in that house his daughter Sophronia and the Rev. Charles Thorn were married by Rev. Thomas McClelland, the first Methodist preacher in the valley, who was a frequent visitor there.

All of the land now comprising the boroughs of Osborn, Sewickley, and Edgeworth, with an immense outlying territory, lay within Pine Township, which was created in 1796 out of Pitt township which included all of the county land west of the Allegheny River and north of the Ohio as far as Lake Erie. Out of Pine was cut Ohio Township in 1803, and in 1853 a portion of Ohio Township was set apart as Sewickley Borough. The Township of Sewickley was not taken from Ohio Township until a year or so later.

Among the early settlers who bought tracts of land around the present borough was James Park, who purchased 205 acres, much of which now makes up Osborn borough. William McLaughlin, great-grandfather of Mrs. P. D. Nicols, bought a tract in 1798, lying in what was later to become Sewickley Township. He was one of the pioneer Scotch-Irish who came from the East over the mountains by Conestoga wagon. Frederick Merriman, who had been a soldier in Wayne's Legion, was a squatter on the McLaughlin land. He afterwards bought 300 acres, more or less, the consideration being a gun, an iron kettle, and a sled. He claims to have had a prior offer for the same gun of forty acres of land in Alleghenytown—the land that is now occupied by the City Hall and the Carnegie Library. "Surely a valuable gun!" as one chronicler remarks. Robert Linn was another Ulsterman, who settled on a neighboring farm and whose descendants are among the old Sewickley families. William Larimore came, it is said, as early as 1793, and took up a farm in what is now Leet Township. A neighbor of his was Nathan McPherson. These are Sewickley names today. Rev. Thomas McClelland in 1809 or 1810, then in his seventieth year, bought a farm about six miles north of the present borough, which remained in the family many years. The price he paid was $1.25 an acre. James Moore, known as Commodore Moore, was the most extensive landowner on the Sewickley hills, his farm comprising some 1200 acres. The Murray and Besterman farms are a part of Moore's land.

The first collection of houses from which the village of Sewickley was evolved naturally grew up on the Pittsburgh and Beaver road. This road was in existence in 1778, and closely follows an old Indian trail leading from the Forks of the Ohio to the northwest country. General Anthony Wayne made a military road of it in 1792, when he led his Legion from Fort Pitt to Logstown, there to drill his men in preparation for a campaign against the hostile Indians, the success of which practically opened the entire region for settlement by the white men. Legionville station on the railroad takes its name from that military camp. Other trails intersected this, coming down our present Waterworks and Blackburn roads and connecting with the great Warriors' Branch trail beyond Frankfort, in Beaver County—the Indians crossing the river at Stoops Ferry by canoe.

The original Hoey farm lay on both sides of the Beaver Road. A portion of it passed to John Hoey and from him to John Little in 1832. The John Hoey homestead stood at what is now the corner of Beaver and Walnut streets. As the village grew, a general store became a necessity, and this was supplied by Robert and James Green, brothers, who began business in a log house on the Beaver Road, just about where

Grimes Street commences. Robert bought land of John Little and built the small frame house on Beaver Road that stood until a few years ago in the corner of the Willock lot, almost in front of the residence of Mr. S. G. Cooper, No. 202 Beaver Street. The Greens' descendants are still large property holders in the central part of the town. Robert continued to keep store for many years, although his brother James went back to his former home in the East. The population to whose necessities he ministered was scattered throughout the township, and had grown in number from 832, in 1810, to 1631, in 1840, according to the figures in Daniel Rupp's *History of Western Pennsylvania*. The community enjoyed a healthy growth. While in 1836 there were but 103 voters in Ohio Township*, a territory which extended from Glenfield to Big Sewickley and some ten miles back from the river, in 1846 the village consisted of thirty houses dotted here and there for a distance of more than a mile, with two churches, a Methodist and a Presbyterian. In 1837 John Garrison opened another store, at his home which stood on Beaver Road where Mr. Hegner's establishment now is, No. 429. Tracy & Schofield for many years had a wagon-shop on the site of Miller's shoe store, No. 503 Beaver Street, where wagons were made for the government during the Mexican War.

Long before the first country store came into existence a church building had been erected. This was a log house built in 1818 beside Hoey's Run, on Division Street, where Challis's yard now is. The first sermon preached in that modest structure was by the Rev. Michael Law, pastor of the church of Montour, across the river. This log building was used many years as a church, then until 1846 as a public school; later it was removed to Fife Street (now Blackburn Avenue), where it became a carpenter shop; and was finally demolished in 1876 when Centennial Avenue was opened.

The erection of this church building did not, of course, mark the first public worship held in the valley. Long before,

*See list at the end of this article.

A HISTORICAL SKETCH 19

THE LOG CHURCH (1818)

as early as 1797 or 1798, the Rev. Francis Reno, an Episcopalian, conducted occasional services in Sewickley Bottom, and continued to do so at intervals until after 1809. Rev. McClelland, a Methodist minister, came in 1808 or 1809 and preached at the house of Jesse Fisher who lived on Daniel Leet's farm, near the site of the old Shields mill on Little Sewickley Creek, below Beaver Road. A few years later, prior to 1823, a frame building was erected as a preaching place on the hill just beyond the old mill. At a later date services were held in the little brick house which was built in 1826 by Mr. Shields, for school, prayer-meetings, and general church purposes, on the hill just opposite his house. This building is still standing, near Mr. D. Leet Wilson's residence. The itinerant Methodist preachers found hospitable entertainment at the home of Mr. and Mrs. Shields, across the way. Services were frequently held in private houses, barns, or in the woods. Mr. John Way, in his paper *The Olden Time in Sewickley*, mentions several such meeting-places: Thomas Hoey's barn which stood on the south side of the Beaver Road, about where Mr. Albert Moore now lives (No. 328 Beaver Street); Mr. Beer's barn, about the corner of Beaver and Peebles streets; Jackson's barn on the lower side of the Beaver Road, about opposite the old stone house just beyond Little Sewickley Creek. "Gradually," he says, "these various points were given up, and the people seem by common consent to have picked upon a beautiful oak grove on Mrs. Addy Beer's place, on Hoey's Run . . . there in the summer seasons they met to hear the gospel." A forty-year lease of this oak grove was secured and the first church erected, in 1818, as stated above. Here beginning on June 1, 1822, the Rev. John Andrews preached to a Presbyterian congregation, serving as stated supply here and at the larger Fairmount church at David Duff's on Big Sewickley, until 1831 or 1832. The two churches grew during his pastorate from twenty-seven communicants to a total of one hundred and twenty-eight.

Prior to 1837 there was no regular Methodist preaching within the present borough limits, though an occasional itinerant preacher held services in the log church on Hoey's Run. It was largely through the efforts of John R. Garrison that the first regular preaching was established in 1837 or 1838. In 1839, when the Rev. John White, father of Judge J. W. F. White, was preacher on the circuit, the first Methodist church was erected, a frame building which stood on the site of the present church fronting on Broad Street. This was succeeded in 1853 by a brick structure, with the first church bell in the valley, installed seven years later. The present building, on the site of the first, was dedicated in 1884. It cost, with the brick chapel and accessories, about $45,000, of which $15,000 came to it by the will of Rev. Charles Thorn, son-in-law of Thomas Hoey. Upon the erection of the brick chapel, fronting on Thorn Street, the old original frame church was removed and now forms a part of the Campney store and dwelling, No. 425 Beaver Street.

In 1860 St. James Roman Catholic church was organized and a lot bought on Walnut Street where the present brick building (now concrete faced) was begun a few years later, succeeding the frame structure in which services were first held. St. Stephen's Episcopal church dates from the year 1863, when the corner stone was laid. Rev. Mr. Ten Broeck was the first rector. This building gave way to the present stone church in 1894. The parish house was built in 1911. In 1864 the United Presbyterians effected an organization and held services in the Methodist church until their own house of worship was completed. It stood on Broad Street, where there is now the double dwelling-house numbered 327 and 329. Rev. W. A. MacKenzie was called in 1865. This property was sold by the congregation and the stone church built on Beaver Street, opposite the head of Peebles, in 1896. The Baptists began holding services in 1873 in Mozart Hall, over Chamberlin's store at the corner of Broad and Beaver streets. They built their church at Beaver and Grimes streets in 1889, where Rouzer's wagon shop and later a roller-skating rink had stood.

Let us leave church history now and turn to other activities, retracing our steps somewhat. Being on one of the main lines of travel to the West, Sewickley boasted of several hotels in the early days. John Little's tavern, sometimes called the Half Way House, from its being midway between Pittsburgh and Beaver, stood in an open space on the Beaver Road where Little Street now begins. Another hostelry in the neighborhood was Fife's, across the road, at the corner of the present Grove Street. This was kept by John Fife, grandfather of Dr. Grimes. It was a brick building, afterwards occupied by the Rev. Joseph Travelli's academy. It was burned down in 1851 and when rebuilt many of the original bricks were used. These gave the walls a peculiar spotted appearance which caused the building to be dubbed "the leprosy house." Mr. Fife married a daughter of Thomas Hoey and built for his home, in 1834, the little log house, afterwards weatherboarded, which stood until 1904 on the north side of Beaver Street on

THE THOMAS BEER HOMESTEAD

the property now owned by Mr. A. L. Lowrie (No. 43). This cottage for years was pointed out as the oldest house in Sewickley. There Mr. Hoey died, in 1838.

Mr. Thomas Beer's homestead on the river bank (built about 1805) was a port of call for travelers going west by way of the river. It was sometimes called the Old Beer Inn. The Beer tavern was a stopping place not only for the keelboatmen but for emigrants and travelers. John Melish, an Englishman, voyaging by skiff down the Ohio in October, 1811, undoubtedly refers to Thomas Beer's inn when he writes as follows: "The afternoon was clear, warm and pleasant and we had an agreeable sail, during which we passed several islands, to a small tavern on the right hand twelve miles from Pittsburgh where we stopped for the night." About a quarter of a mile back from the river and just off the Beaver Road was the Park Inn, kept by James Park, Sr., who built it, also in 1805. This old stone house is still standing. John and Elizabeth Mitchell bought it from the Parks in 1864 and lived in it until 1899, when it was sold to Mr. Joseph Lambie, its present owner. The name of the original landholder is preserved in Park's Run and Park's Hollow, the latter now generally known as Glen Mitchell, a name said to have been suggested by Dr. Bittinger.

In the days of long ago, when Sewickley was a quiet little village and not a residential suburb of Pittsburgh, this community had a character all its own. Life in this beautiful valley then surely must have had a touch of the idyllic. While the glamour which hovers over the good old times may blind us to what was sordid and difficult in the daily round of those who preceded us, still it is certainly true that their lives were more tranquil, their pleasures simpler, and their wants fewer than ours. Think of the quiet which had not yet been disturbed by the clatter of the railroad or the insistent horn of the automobile! Picture the landscape untouched by smoke, the valley still beautiful with much of its original growth of chestnut, oak, and maple, and the village streets not yet made unsightly by telegraph poles! A primitive little town it was,

EDGEWORTH FEMALE SEMINARY
From a lithograph in a prospectus of the school, dated 1838.

with streets unpaved, uncurbed, and unlighted, marked by board fences and here and there a board sidewalk whose planks, laid lengthwise, were prone to warp and turn up at the ends, tripping the unwary. These boards were evidently "seconds," as they contained the auger holes through which wooden pegs had been driven to hold together the rafts by which the lumber had been floated down from the upper river.

The only means of communication with the city was by occasional stage-coach or steamboat and yet Sewickley was not out of touch with the world nor unknown beyond its boundaries, for the fame of its schools spread its name far and wide and attracted to it young men and women from all parts of the country. The boys' academy and the Edgeworth Seminary, which flourished in the days before the Civil War, lent quite an academic air to the community.

Mrs. Mary Olver, an accomplished and stately Englishwoman, founded the Edgeworth Female Seminary in 1825, naming it for the novelist, Maria Edgeworth. It was first located in Pittsburgh, but soon afterwards it was removed to Braddock's Field, and in 1836 to the Sewickley valley, where it occupied a brick building to the south of the Beaver Road and a short distance west of what is now Edgeworth Lane, then called Seminary Lane. In its prospectus (of 1838) Sewickley is described as "an eligible location on the north bank of the Ohio River, near the village of Economy. It has regular and free communication with the city both by the river and the great public road leading to Beaver and Cleveland. By stage or steamboat the distance [to the city] may be traveled in a few hours." Some years later the railroad adopted the name for a station in the vicinity and today the memory of Mrs. Olver's seminary is preserved in the name of the borough of Edgeworth where the school was located, though Olver Street, passing back of the seminary, has been changed to Oliver. In its school-room the Sewickley Presbyterian Church was organized, by order of the Presbytery of

1860

SEWICKLEYVILLE

ALLEGHENY CO. PA.

Ohio, on February 17, 1838, by Rev. John Williamson Nevin and Rev. Joseph Reed. In this organization no one took a livelier or more active interest than Mrs. Olver. Upon her death, in 1842, the seminary was closed and it remained so until 1846, when it was reopened by Rev. Daniel E. Nevin, who conducted it successfully for six and a half years. Following Mr. Nevin as principal were Prof. Samuel R. Williams (1852-4), Rev. Henry R. Wilson, and Rev. Aaron Williams. The career of the seminary ended with the destruction of the two wooden wings of the building by fire, on February 11, 1865. The central part, which was of stone, remained and is standing today, having been remodeled several times. It is now the residence of Mr. J. Wilkinson Elliott. Hon. Morrison Foster, brother of Stephen C. Foster, lived there for a number of years.

The Sewickley Academy for boys was opened in 1838, by John B. Champ, an Englishman, and William M. Nevin, a brother of Rev. D. E. Nevin, in 'Squire Way's Brick House, on Beaver Road, and it soon attained a reputation as a school of high character. The following advertisement appears in *Harris's Pittsburgh Directory*, for the year 1839.

"NEVIN & CHAMPS CLASSICAL and COMMERCIAL school for Boys: on the OHIO River, fourteen miles below Pittsburgh. Terms, $75. per season of five months; half to be paid in ADVANCE."

Upon the removal from the valley of Messrs. Champ and Nevin (1841), the former to Michigan and the latter to accept the professorship of English at Marshall College, Mercersburg, Pa. (which, continued in the united Franklin & Marshall College, he held for fifty years), the academy was closed for a while, but was reopened in 1842 by Rev. Joseph S. Travelli in the Fife house on Beaver Street, in the village. Under Mr. Travelli the school prospered and became more widely known. As the river was the natural highway from the South, many students were drawn from that section, some coming even from as far as New Orleans. Mrs. S. M. Glenn, a daughter

REV. JOSEPH S. TRAVELLI

of Mr. Travelli, tells of the barrels of sugar-cane and other home products which used to come up the river by steamboat for the Southern boys who remained at the academy over the Christmas holidays. For weeks the whole school enjoyed the luxury of chewing sugar-cane.

When the Fife house was burned, in 1851, the academy was moved to the building now the Park Place Hotel. Two wings were added to an old building which had stood on the Hoey property and the premises adapted to school requirements. Here Mr. Travelli conducted the academy until 1864. The Civil War made serious inroads in its attendance, so many of the boys hurrying off to their homes in the South.

Miss Ellis, in her *Lights and Shadows of Sewickley Life*, gives a picture of the academy boys and the girls from the seminary walking decorously and demurely to church under the watchful eyes of their sedate teachers. The girls occupied the gallery in the little brick Presbyterian church, where they were reasonably removed as a source of distraction to the boys.

President Zachary Taylor's passage through the village in 1848, on his way to the West, was an exciting event in the lives of the boys and girls, and of their elders as well.

The party left Pittsburgh on the morning of August 31. The paper stated that they would dine at Economy and lodge at Beaver; Sewickley was therefore prepared in advance. In the Pittsburgh *Gazette* an interesting account of the episode is given. To quote:

"Two of the citizens of Sewickley met the President on his approach to the Valley, last Tuesday, and invited him in behalf of the institute and the community to visit the Edgeworth Ladies' School. They also handed him the following invitation from the pupils of that institution.

'DEAR GENERAL:

We wish very much to see you, and delicacy forbids our running to the roadside to gaze upon you whilst passing. Could you not drive into the Seminary grounds, and pause a few minutes, in front of the porch, and we will always gratefully remember your kindness. That you, of whom we have heard so much during your celebrated career in Mexico, of whom our fathers and brothers talked so hopefully in the recent election time, and now too, our President, should pass our gate without our having the privilege of seeing you, would fill us with lasting regret. Do, dear General, permit us to salute you here, as you pass, and please convey our compliments to the Governor of our Commonwealth, who, we understand, is travelling with you, we hope to greet him in your company.

Yours respectfully,
THE YOUNG LADIES
OF EDGEWORTH ACADEMY.'"

"As gallant as he was fearless," to quote from another writer, "Old Zach could not resist this appeal. He capitulated at once, and in company with Governor Johnston, drove into the grounds where they were met by the Rev. Joseph S. Travelli and Rev. Daniel E. Nevin, headmasters respectively of the academic schools for boys and girls. He was formally introduced by Dr. Nevin, and given a most hearty reception. Both the distinguished callers made pretty speeches, the students signifying their delight by round after round of cheers. In the course of Governor Johnston's remarks he stated that he had always had a soft spot in his heart for the Edgeworth School, as his wife, the best woman in the world, was a graduate of the institution. This was received with demonstrations of approval, particularly by the young ladies. As the party drove away, the girls continued their cheers, and remained on the porch waving their handkerchiefs until the cavalcade was out of sight on its journey to Beaver."

Until the year 1840 the village had no officially established name. It had enjoyed various appellations—in the sense in which one is said to enjoy ill health. *Oppotongo* was one of the earliest, an Indian name, used within the recollection of Mr. Elias Reno, now living. This name is mentioned by Rev. Daniel E. Nevin in a poem in which he narrates an Indian legend of the valley. *Fifetown* was the name perhaps as generally used as any, in honor of the numerous family of Fifes. *Bowling Green* had been favored by some. *Dogtown, Contention,* and *The Devil's Race Track* are regrettable memories reminiscent, probably, of the days of the keelboatmen and squatters along the river who once formed a considerable part of the community. These "hardy frontiersmen," as we delight to call them, were in reality a lawless, roistering, and illiterate lot.

The name *Sewickley Bottom* came to be applied exclusively to that portion of the valley lying near Little Sewickley Creek, and a post-office so designated had been established there as early as 1825, Mr. David Shields assuming the duties of postmaster, in combination with those of storekeeper, in the front room of his house, now the home of Mrs. L. Halsey Williams, his granddaughter. Finally, in the fall of the year 1840, a meeting of the citizens was called for the purpose of definitely deciding upon a name for the village, at which *Sewickleyville* was chosen, the termination "ville" being used as properly distinguishing the more closely settled portion of the valley from that known as the "Bottom." The name was hailed with bonfires and great rejoicings, with which we can readily sympathize in view of the names that we escaped. Old postmarks show that the name *Sewickleyville* received the sanction of the post-office authorities, but when the village was incorporated in 1853 the borough was called simply "Sewickley," though the longer form continued in popular use for some years, possibly because the post-office, established in 1851, was so called until 1871. Mr. John Way, afterwards of Lisbon, Ohio, was the first appointed postmaster.

The year 1851 was marked by another event of greater importance than the establishing of the post-office. In that year the Ohio and Pennsylvania Railroad was opened and the first train passed through Sewickley. July 4 had been set as the date for the great event, and the program was followed out even though passenger coaches were not yet ready for service. Gravel cars with improvised board seats were attached to the engine and the run was made to Economy, the end of the line, where the intrepid passengers were regaled by the Economites with a feast of celebration. Soon a regular passenger service of two trains a day was established between Pittsburgh and the valley, and gradually, as the service increased, the change from village to city suburb took place.

Of course the railroad met with opposition. Such innovations always do. It was not the stage-coach drivers, as in England, who made chief objection, but property owners who feared that their land would depreciate in value or their cows cease to give milk if frightened by the terrible steam-engine. Mr. Ezra Young, advocating the introduction of a trolley line at a meeting held recently in Edgeworth, told the following:

SEWICKLEY'S FIRST POST OFFICE
Beaver Street west of Chestnut

"Objections will be raised, as they always are, to any enterprise that is intended to benefit a community. Being one of the oldest living residents of the valley, I well remember how the introduction of steam railroads here was bitterly opposed in the early 'fifties. My own ancestors, the Andersons, then living on a farm that took in the land now covered by the town of Leetsdale, were among the most bitter opponents. They were somewhat relieved, however, when Mrs. David Shields came to see my grandmother and said, 'Don't be alarmed, Auntie; the Economites and Mr. Shields are opposed to the railroad and it won't be built.'"

The railroad was built, however, and the first Sewickley station was a rough frame building which stood on the south side of the single track, a little east of Chestnut Street, about where the freight station now is. This building was afterwards moved across the track and used as a combination council-chamber and village lockup. The second station, a brick one, occupied the same site as the first, while the third, the present building on the north side of the tracks and east of Broad Street, was built in 1885.

By the mid-century Sewickley had grown to be a village of some five hundred inhabitants and desired to become a borough. Accordingly, on April 8, 1853, there was presented to the grand jury a petition of a majority of the freeholders and a majority of the legal voters within "the present limits of the Borough of Sewickley who are desirous of being regularly incorporated as a Borough and forming a separate election and School District." (It will be noticed that the petitioners elsewhere refer to themselves as "the citizens of Sewickleyville.") Of the eighty-two signers, sixty-one were freeholders and twenty-one were "voters not freeholders.*" The petition having been considered by the grand jury and the incorporation recommended, a decree was made by the court on July 6, 1853. These proceedings are found of record in Deed Book, vol. 108 at page 122, and not the least interesting part of the record is the map of the proposed borough

*The list will be found at the end of this article.

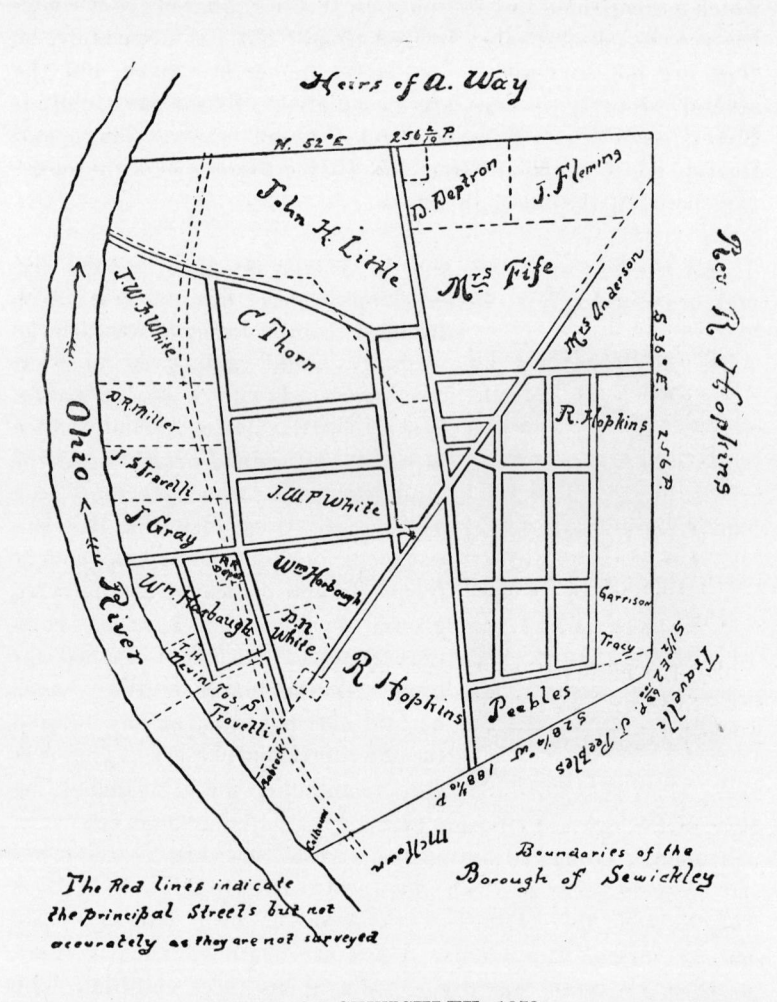

MAP OF SEWICKLEY, 1853.
The original, drawn in two colors, is part of the Charter petition.

which accompanied the petition. In this first plan of the borough the streets are indicated by red lines "but not accurately, as they are not surveyed." No street names are given, but the several property owners are designated. Broad and Walnut Streets seem not to have been cut through between Thorn and Beaver, while Division Street has all the dignity of a thoroughfare between the borough limits.

An election was held, and on August 30, 1853, council met and organized. Rev. Robert Hopkins, the first burgess (Mrs. Rudolph Lipp's father), was a large property holder and lived in what was afterwards known as the Watson house, on Blackburn Avenue, which he built. He owned nearly all of the land within the borough limits east of Division Street, including the cemetery property, which was bought from him and dedicated as a burying ground on November 1, 1860. Hopkins Street, of course, is named for him. Another large section, which he laid out in a plan of lots, he sold to individual purchasers. This was the triangular piece bounded by Beaver, Peebles and Division Streets, "situated in Ohio Township, Allegheny County, adjoining the town of Sewickley," which was surveyed as early as 1849, and recorded in 1851, in Plan Book vol. 1, page 189. Other portions of the town had been laid out by various individuals. Upon the death of Thomas Hoey, in 1838, his estate was divided among his three children, John Hoey, Mrs. Fife and Mrs. Thorn. Mrs. Thorn's portion lay south of Beaver Street and east of Hoey's Run, and was sold to Messrs. Gray and Chadwick, who laid out the principal streets, which were afterwards confirmed, though the sale was set aside on account of certain legal complications. John Hoey took as his share the land south of Beaver Street and west of the

REV. ROBERT HOPKINS

run, selling it later to John H. Little, who subdivided it; while that part of the farm to the north of the Beaver Road which remained unsold went to Mrs. Fife. In 1837 John R. Garrison had bought the triangle bounded by Beaver, Division and Fife Streets and laid out lots fronting on Beaver Street, on some of which he built houses. In 1860 a three-cornered section of Mrs. Thorn's holdings was surveyed for her son-in-law, William Harbaugh, by Hays & Darley, and put on record in Plan Book vol. 3, page 180. This lies between Chestnut, Harbaugh and Division Streets, just across the line from the Rev. Hopkins plan.

In 1856 the first official survey and map of the borough was made by Alexander Hays (afterwards General Hays), the original document being now on file in the borough engineer's office. This plan (which seems not to have been put on record) shows thirty-one streets, a curious feature being that none runs directly through from the river to the hill, a condition that will be changed only when the new bridge is connected with Broad Street. All of the streets laid out at that time were confined to what are now the first and third wards, while Beaver Street was the only one extending west of the present Blackburn Avenue and Walnut Street. It is interesting to note some of the original street names. Bank Street, east of Chestnut, was called *Railroad Street; Clark Street*, between Peebles and Logan, is now a part of Thorn Street; *Vine Street* is now part of Frederick Avenue; *Locust Street,* between Nevin Avenue and Division Street, forms part of Centennial. *Wheelbarrow Lane* is Boundary Street now; *Mechanic's Street* is part of Logan; *Gray Street* is changed to Nevin Avenue, and *Fife Street* to Blackburn Avenue. Broad Street ran from Bank to Beaver Street. To go up the hill above Beaver, one passed through *Short Alley* (now Hegner Alley) to Division Street and thence by *Crooked Street* (which accounts for the still remaining name of the not-far-distant Straight Street), to Hopkins. Between Woods's (now A. C. Walker's) drug store and Reibert's shop, which occupied the site of the First National Bank, there was a fenced-off open lot through which Broad Street was eventually carried, in 1878, the extension north of Beaver being originally called *Lincoln Avenue.*

This map of 1856 shows us the village practically as it was in the days of the Civil War.

Of those days it is hard to draw an adequate picture. The alternation of excitement and grief, of discouragement and hope, which marked those four bitter years cannot be fully appreciated by us of a younger generation. At the outbreak of the war the young men of the Sewickley valley responded loyally and eagerly to their country's call. A company was organized and drilling began in the new Presbyterian church, the present building, which had just been roofed and floored. On July 6, 1861, the company left for Philadelphia and was mustered into service July 11 as Company G of the 28th Regiment of Pennsylvania Volunteers. On the Sunday before they left, the soldier boys attended morning service in the Presbyterian church and evening service in the Methodist, walking two by two up the aisle to their allotted seats. On the forenoon of the day of their departure, in the presence of a large gathering swords were presented to Captain Conrad U. Meyers and to Lieutenants William C. Shields and John I. Nevin, J. W. F. White, Esq., making the presentation speech. Each man in the company at the same time was presented with a New Testament and an appropriate address was made by Rev. James Allison. Then followed the good-byes— and the days of anxious waiting. Six months from the day the company left Sewickley the first break in its ranks occurred, in the death of Private A. Jackson Gray at Camp Goodman, Point of Rocks, Maryland. The second death was that of Joseph Moore, brother of Mr. Albert Moore, in March, 1862. Then came the dark days following Antietam in September, and the never-to-be-forgotten funeral services held in the Presbyterian church over the bodies of James D. Travelli, John D. Tracy and William C. Ritchey, who were killed in that battle. Other young men from the valley enlisted, and meanwhile, week after week, the girls met in the church to sew for the soldier boys. The memories of the Civil War which are associated with this building are indeed a precious heritage.

Shortly after the close of that great struggle, the Soldiers' Monument was placed in the cemetery, commemorating those

THE SOLDIERS' MONUMENT

who gave their lives for the Union. The following names are inscribed thereon: "Killed in battle. Lieutenant Wm. C. Shields, Wm. Banks, John D. Tracy, Wm. Painter, James D. Travelli, Robert White, Wm. C. Ritchey, Theodore Webb, Robert Johnston, Wm. Wharton, Thomas Smith, Moses Sherman. Died of Wounds and Diseases. Captain Alexander McKinney, James Scott, James L. Grady, John Park, Albert J. White, Joseph Moore, Andrew J. Gray, Henry M. Rhodes, Wm. I. Nevin, Thomas A. Hill, W. H. Forrester, Harry Black, G. W. Forrester, Alex. Black, James Grimes, L. B. Gainer." Today there are buried in our cemetery upwards of eighty veterans of the war, the roll of honor lengthening as the years thin the ranks of survivors.

In the decade of the 'seventies Sewickley made material advancement. In 1879 the second survey of the town was made, which shows the development of all territory within the borough limits, the laying out of streets in the second ward, with a number of changes in names, widths, and locations of the original streets. In 1872 the old White and Harbaugh farm of twenty-five acres, a part of the Charles Thorn property, bounded by Bank and Thorn, Little and Walnut streets, had been bought by David Sands and James Adair and by them laid out in a plan of lots which were sold at auction the following year. This was the largest and most valuable tract of land ever offered, among the several additions made to the borough. In the naming of the streets in this plan the children of the Adair and Sands families were remembered, Alec Adair (called *Elwick* by one of his little brothers), Frederick Sands, Emery Sands, and Henry Adair lent their first names to as many streets, while the name *Rose* was given to the alley adjoining Thorn Street as an appropriate juxtaposition. As Mr. Adair once remarked: "No alley was ever more fragrant."

Within this decade the borough made other valuable acquisitions: a library, a waterworks and a fire company.

The Sewickley Library had its beginning in a meeting held February 7, 1873, in Mozart Hall (the hall at the corner of Beaver and Broad streets, now used by the Knights of Pythias). It was a meeting of "a few young men of the borough," and was held "for the purpose of establishing a Reading Room and Library Association." Quoting from a paper by Mr. Bayard H. Christy:

"Some persons may be interested to know who 'a few young men of the borough' were, forty years ago, and I take from the minute book the names of the persons who at the first meeting subscribed themselves active members of the Association which was then being formed. They were E. R. Kramer, F. A. Myers, John Dickson, William Dickson, John Thomas, S. A. Chamberlin, R. Boobyer, S. C. Ritchey, S. Y. Anderson, W. A. McElwain, C. Fleming, Jr., and John Lent.

"The new enterprise was called the Young Men's Library Association, and the organization was effected by obtaining a charter and adopting a constitution. A board of ten direc-

40 THE VILLAGE OF SEWICKLEY

Robert Watson

Wm. Harbaugh

Theodore H. Nevin

J. W. F. White

D. N. White

SEWICKLEY'S FIRST WATER COMMISSIONERS

tors was provided for and, at the first election of directors and officials, the following board was chosen and organized: John Way, Jr., president; William Dickson, vice president; E. R. Kramer, secretary; John Thomas, treasurer; and in addition the board of directors included John McElwain, Kidd Fleming, C. T. Harbaugh, Rev. S. B. Moore, George H. Christy, and C. F. Nevin. Two auditors were elected, F. M. Hutchinson and William Harbaugh.

"This board of directors, with few changes, continued to serve during seven years, from the beginning of the enterprise to the time when its property was turned over to the control of the school board, and the Library as a private venture came to an end. Mr. Way continued to be the president through all the period and Mr. Kramer the secretary."

To Joseph W. Warren great credit is due for his untiring efforts in raising money to finance the library. His dramatic entertainments, given year after year, were well attended and hailed with enthusiasm—to the great benefit of the fund.

For its water Sewickley had been dependent upon a number of deep wells and cisterns scattered throughout the village. The need of a more adequate supply led to the holding of a public meeting in Mozart Hall on June 15, 1872, where a resolution was passed calling upon council to appoint a water commission. On June 24, council named Messrs. T. H. Nevin, D. N. White, Robert Watson, J. W. F. White, and William Harbaugh, and made an appropriation of $500 to cover the cost of preliminary surveys, etc. The outcome of this action was the purchase of the beautiful tract of land whose springs long sufficed to supply the needs of the village, and whose advantages as a public park, aside from its utilitarian value, have proved the wisdom and foresight of the first water commission.

Following the completion of the waterworks, in 1874, a volunteer fire company was organized, at a meeting held also in Mozart Hall on the evening of April 6, 1876. David R. Scott was chosen foreman and Alex. McHenry and Hiram Lake assistant foremen. Upon council's declining to make an appropriation for the purchase of equipment, the necessary money was raised by subscription, largely through the efforts of the burgess, George W. Cochran. In recognition of his services and enthusiastic support, the name *Cochran Hose Company* was adopted. The fire company remained an independent organization until 1879, when the apparatus was presented to the borough. It was housed for many years in the little building on Division Street between Beaver and Chestnut, now the Reibert property; thence it was moved to the old Neely blacksmith shop at the corner of Chestnut and Washington streets, where it remained until the completion of the town hall in 1910, where our volunteer firemen were at last provided with comfortable and adequate quarters.

The first fire to which the company responded was at the Merriman house, up the Waterworks Road; but little could be done, as it was far from any fire-plug. When Reibert's store, on the site of the First National Bank, caught fire, in April, 1878, the boys had their first opportunity to show their mettle. Though the store was burnt out, "the operation was successful," in that the fire was kept from spreading to Ellis's shoe store and other frame buildings adjoining. A spirited oil painting of the exciting event was made by John Drynan, which may be seen today on the wall of his office, No. 437 Beaver Street.

In 1878 Capt. J. Sharp McDonald, Stuart S. Colville, and W. F. Speer leased an old sawmill property at the foot of Ferry Street on the river bank and turned it into a boat-yard. In April, 1879, the first boat was launched, the steamer *Butte,* destined for the upper Missouri trade. The next was the *James Lee,* a side-wheel packet for the lower Mississippi; then they built the *Wyoming* for the Pittsburgh-St. Louis line and the *Florida,* a side-wheeler, for the coast trade between Savannah and Jacksonville. Several towboats followed, of which the *W. W. O'Neil* was one. Seventeen hulls in all were constructed, before the yard was wiped out by fire, in 1883. A part of the old boat-yard site is now occupied by the John B. Semple fuse and tracer factory.

The feeling of neighborliness which existed between Sewickley and the quaint German village of Economy, "down the road," was pleasantly shown in a series of annual visits paid to us in the 'seventies by the Economites, who chose the winter time for their excursions and appeared in a procession of sleds headed by their famous band. All Sewickley turned out to welcome them, and a reception was held in Choral Hall, followed by a band concert tendered by our guests. In 1879, by way of returning the compliment, "a sleighing party of four hundred" as the newspapers reported it, set out from Sewickley, to invade the quiet precincts of the Harmonists. Friday, January 17, was the day, and the children of the public school in twenty-three bob-sleds, accompanied by the school directors, teachers, military aides on horseback, and two bands, formed the cavalcade. It was truly an invasion. No announcement had preceded it, and yet the jolly party met with the warmest welcome at the hands of the sedate Economites. The town hall was thrown open and the visitors regaled with apples and ginger cakes, while the rafters rang with the music of the bands. The return journey was made without mishap and, in the language of the country newspaper, "a good time was had by all." What the effect was on the Economites, history does not record, but the exchange of amenities between the villages seems to have ended with this children's crusade.

The principal event of the 'eighties was, of course, the erection and dedication of the new Methodist church, in 1884. Through the activity of Judge J. W. F. White the sum of $1,200 was collected to purchase the town clock which was placed in the church tower that year. Of this sum, all but $379 was contributed by members of that congregation, although the clock is an object of general public benefit.

In a mere historical sketch, as this paper of necessity must be, it is impossible to go into the details of the social and business life of the community, and a bare catalogue of the numerous organizations which have sprung into existence

THE OLD MUSIC HALL AT ECONOMY

in the past thirty years would be uninteresting. In an exhaustive history of our town, which it is to be hoped some abler historian may one day write, such details as the founding and personnel of the first Masonic lodge and of the other fraternal and social organizations, the establishment of our banks, of the Young Men's Christian Association, of the hospital, and so forth, may profitably be considered. An interesting chapter would be devoted to the various newspapers which flourished at different periods, some the creatures of a day, others with long and useful careers. The Sewickley Athletic Association, founded in 1882, and enjoying a deserved popularity for more than fifteen years, would be given a large place in such a chronicle. With what pleasure do we not look back to the activities of those days at the Athletic Grounds, on Mrs. R. H. Davis's property on Nevin Avenue! This is now a choice residential section; the old ball-field and tennis courts, the bowling alley, and even the spring having been wiped out and the creek pushed aside, to make way for streets and dwellings.

Let us hope that some day a full and adequate history of Sewickley may be written. Meanwhile, a word about our schools should not be omitted from this sketch. The first school was held in the old log church on Division Street, built in 1818, and continued there until 1846. In its one window, a small opening between the logs, oiled paper served instead of glass. The teacher was a Mr. Scott. In 1848 the first real school-house was built, a brick and frame building, also on Division Street, at a point near the present intersection of Broad Street and Centennial Avenue. This continued in use down to 1862, and some of the pupils of that school we have still with us, among whom may be mentioned William Dickson and G. Fred Muller. One of their schoolmates, C. Stanley Rinehart, who attained world-wide celebrity as an artist and illustrator, gave promise even in those days of his future fame in his illustrations of the text of the school paper, *The Privateer,* which was put forth by the students. The present school property on Chestnut Street was bought in 1860, the frontage on Broad Street a little later, and a brick building of four

SEWICKLEY'S FIRST SCHOOL HOUSE (1848)

rooms erected which, with several additions, continued in use from 1862 till 1893, when it was destroyed by fire. The present building was put up in 1894. The attendance has grown from a mere handful in the 'forties to an enrollment of 850 pupils in the grammar and high schools of today.

In 1896 a cavalry company was organized in the valley through the efforts of Capt. David Shields, Mr. Edward P. Coffin, and others, but for several reasons it had disbanded when, in 1898, the Spanish war fever struck Sewickley and the Sewickley Troop was permanently organized. Efforts were made to have the company sent to the front, but as this proved impracticable many of the members enlisted and saw active service in the 14th and 18th Regiments of Pennsylvania Volunteers and in Battery B. The boys in the battery were the only ones that had the good fortune to be sent out of the country. It was their guns that were trained upon the Spaniards in the mountains of Porto Rico, awaiting the signal to open battle, when news of the peace protocol was received, and the war was over.

* * * *

Our historical sketch now brings us down to extremely modern times, of which it is difficult to write with the proper perspective. On the whole, it seems best not to attempt to carry it further but to let this imperfect review of Sewickley's past suffice, leaving to some future scribe the task of writing the history of the Sewickley-Coraopolis bridge and the celebrations attending its opening, in the fall of 1911.

Sewickley is now a prosperous and happy community of 4,500 people, flanked on either side by its sister boroughs, Osborn and Edgeworth. May the near future see the three boroughs joined in one, as their community of interests demands that they should be, forming by their union a Greater Sewickley in which we shall take even a greater pride and for which we shall feel in our hearts a stronger allegiance!

February, 1913.

LIST OF VOTERS IN OHIO TOWNSHIP IN 1836

A list of the names of voters at an election held on Tuesday, the 11th day of October, A. D. 1836, at the house of Thomas Hamilton, Ohio Township.

From a document loaned by Mr. William Linn.

William Frazer
Hugh Duff, Esq.
Nicholas Way
Campbell McGlaughlin
Davidson Duff
John Mitchell, Esq.
James Duff, Jr.
Thomas J. Pierson
William Courtny
Edward Crawford
John Scott
John Gillen
John Seaton
William Hamilton
David Dickson
Andrew Gilleland, Jr.
William Long
Nathan McFersen, Sr.
James Gilleland
David Shields
William Jackman
Samuel Baggs
George Merriman
William C. Means
Lewellen Bonem
John Taylor, Sr.
John Means
John Brewer
John McFersen, Jr.
Samuel McFersen
Frederick Merriman, Jr.
Andrew Pinkerton
Nathan McFerson, Jr.
James Brooks
    Campbell Duff (Voted on age)

Robert Anderson, Esq.
Adam Scott
John George
James Merriman, Jr.
Levi Merriman
Thomas Wagener
Samuel Creese
William Sutton
Samuel Merriman, Jr.
John Anderson
Alexander Merriman
Jacob Fry
James Anderson
    (Voted on age)
David Wilkey
John Lauramor
James Park
James Wilkey
William Wagener
Francis Logan
Robert Scott
James Wakefield
William Crawford
Isaac Crawford
William Ritchey
Jackson Gillen
James Crawford
Frederick Merriman
George Stuck
John McFerson, Sr.
Edward O'Neil, Jr.
Edward O'Neil, Sr.
William Duff
Patterson Mitchell

John Stuck
Craven Stevens
Henry Creese
Robert Lin
Thomas Pinkerton
James Duff
James Skiley
Thomas Mitchell
James Laird
Hugh Lin
Wilson Mitchell
John O'Neil
Dr. John Dickson
Samuel Little
Alexander Miller
John Leeser
Thomas Merriman
William Reno
Thomas Hamilton
William Morrow
George Mitchell
John McLaughlin
Alexander McSortin
James McLaughlin
Philip Young
Andrew Creese
John Dickson
Samuel Means
McClelland Hood
James Frey
John R. Garrison
John Creese, Sr.
George Creese
James Duff
Francis Duff

List of Petitioners for Borough Charter
SEWICKLEY, 1853
(Deed Book, vol.108, page 122)

Freeholders

Samuel E. Babcock, John F. White, William Harbaugh, Charles Thorn, David R. Miller, Joseph S. Travelli, E. W. Worthington, John Way, Lewis F. McClelland, Solomon Ague, A. McElwain, Wilson Moor, George F. Rudisill, James P. Mars, T. H. Nevin, D. E. Nevin, John Miller, Joseph Bush, Samuel Morrow, James McClelland, Samuel D. Miller, Charles Miskaeis, William A. Ellis, James Ellis, John Ague, John R. Garrison, James Miller, Robert Hopkins, James McC. Williams, James Allan, Daniel Deputron, William C. Gray, Joseph Craft, James Blackstock, Robert H. Cochran, John Lake, Frederick Ringley, Stephen Dickson, John Norris, Charles Norris, John M. Stevens, Robert Lutle, John C. Little, Baldwin Gray, Philo Goff, John Dickson, Absolom Smith, James Gray, William Miller, Bruce Tracey, Thomas Stevenson, Wylie S. Means, William Sarver, Josiah Winters, Alexander Winters, James Grimes, John Fleming, George Hall, Levi Wade, D. N. White, John Ingram.

Voters Not Freeholders

A. M. Reed, John B. S. Ward, Abraham Miller, James R. Wilson, James Allison, S. T. Garrison, David R. McPherson, T. P. Brown, James W. Stevens, Charles Lake, Watson Moore, G. S. Moore, John Estep, James E. Anderson, Esq., William M. May, John D. Hyke, Robert A. McCray, John Hamilton, George Gray, Albert G. Williams, John Sneed.

ADDY BEER'S GROVE

ADDY BEER'S GROVE

ONE OF THE FIRST PLACES OF PUBLIC WORSHIP

THE old oak tree on Hill Street not far from Blackburn Avenue had long since passed its prime. Shorn of most of its branches, it gave no shade and was a menace and an obstruction to traffic, standing as it did in the middle of the sidewalk, with no compensating advantages either of beauty or of usefulness. So it had to come down to be converted into firewood, leaving only the stump, full nine feet in girth, to await the time when it too shall be removed, the last relic of a noble forest tree, the last vestige of the beautiful grove of which it had once been a part, "Addy Beer's grove," that lay under the hill on which now stands the Valley Hospital. Along the banks of Hoey's Run and grouped about a clear and sparkling spring stood in close array many splendid oaks and chestnuts, a lovely forest glade with open vistas between the great tree boles.

Addy Beer was the widow of Thomas Beer who on April 7th, 1802, had bought from John Vail and Sarah Vail, his wife, for the sum of $1,752.00, a tract of 219 acres lying to the east of what is now Division Street and extending from low water mark on the Ohio River back northward to the hills. On this land Thomas Beer in 1805 built his home, the low frame dwelling on the river bank at Glen Osborne, which was destroyed by fire in 1925, and the very site of which has now disappeared with the shifting of the railroad's right-of-way. Here he lived and made a home for his growing family while keeping tavern for the keelboatmen and travelers who passed up and down the river. Dying in 1809, he left to survive him his widow Addy Beer and nine children (one of them, Abigail, was the wife of James Hoey, another of the earliest settlers here). Addy Beer's farm, the land was then called, and "Addy Beer's grove" the forest-covered tract that became a favorite resort of the sparse inhabitants of the district. For the settlers were few. Along the river bank squatters had here and there made their homes, for the most part a rough and turbulent lot. The two chief landholders of the better sort were Thomas Beer in "Aleppo," and Henry Ulery, a retired sea captain who on April 10th, 1798, had bought from Jonathan Leet for ninety-eight pounds, fifteen shillings the entire 250-acre tract called "Loretto" which lay on the west side of the dividing line between Breading's and Leet's districts. Ulery was the owner also of 25 acres known as "The Ferry" on the other side of the river, for which he had received a patent on February 14, 1793, out of which the Commonwealth reserved to itself "the one-fifth part of all gold and silver ore, to be delivered at the pit's mouth clear of all charges."

In 1810 the cholera threatened, and Ulery and Beer set aside half an acre each as a burying ground. This one-acre plot lay across the line separating their farms, just where the new high school now stands. Naturally the dividing line became a lane, "Graveyard Lane," and, later, Division Street, running due north and south, or nearly so. Leaving the Beer homestead, a walk of something less than a mile through the dense chestnut woods on the lower level and the forest of white oaks farther up brought you to Addy Beer's grove.

Gradually the soberer element of the community increased in numbers and the roistering keelboatmen and riffraff of the river ceased to be the predominant type. The God-fearing folk naturally drew together for Sunday worship, gathering in various places, most frequently in barns, one of which stood about opposite the present United Presbyterian Church, another near the foot of Sand Hill, on the Beaver Road. The sugar camp on the river bank a short distance above Shousetown Lane was another favorite meeting place; but gradually the people by common consent resorted to Addy Beer's grove as the most convenient and pleasant place for Sunday worship.

The comfortable shade of the forest trees and the cool waters of the bubbling spring added physical refreshment to the spiritual satisfaction provided by the religious services. Itinerant preachers held forth here from time to time, ministering to all without regard to sect; but finally the Methodists drew apart and began the erection of a separate house of worship down near

Little Sewickley Creek in the "Sewickley Bottom," as it was called. The Presbyterians took a similar step when, in 1818, they leased the grove from Mrs. Addy Beer for a term of forty years and built, of hewn logs, the first Presbyterian church, wherein one Michael Law is said to have preached the first sermon.

Gradually the ancient oaks surrendered to advancing age and the encroachment of suburban development. The first considerable dwelling erected in the grove was that of Rev. Robert F. Hopkins, in 1850, who two years before had bought 114 acres from the Samuel Peebles estate, successors to the Beer heirs. That house, with an added half story, was known to us of the present generation as the Watson house, and only a year or two ago it gave way to the present lot plan development which now covers the block north of Hill Street and west of Locust Place.

Last of all to yield before the inexorable march of events was that grizzled old veteran whose stump alone remains to mark the location of the old-time meeting place and pleasure ground that was called by the earliest inhabitants of the valley—"Addy Beer's grove."

February, 1928.

CAPTAIN JOHN C. ANDERSON
On His One Hundredth Birthday

OLD SEWICKLEY TAVERNS

REMINISCENCES OF

CAPTAIN JOHN C. ANDERSON

JAMES PARK'S TAVERN

OLD SEWICKLEY TAVERNS

REMINISCENCES OF CAPTAIN JOHN C. ANDERSON IN HIS ONE HUNDREDTH YEAR

No citizen of our Valley was better known or more honored than Captain John C. Anderson, whose one hundredth birthday was celebrated as a community event on January 14, 1928. The following notes of a conversation with him will be of general interest.

* * * *

Passing over the dramatic story of his experiences as a 'Forty-niner and as a pilot for twenty-five years on the Ohio and Cumberland rivers, his early recollections were called forth with particular reference to the hotels that flourished in this vicinity.

"Well," said the Captain, "they were called taverns in those days. There was the one at Haysville. The first proprietor that I know anything about was John Anderson; no relation to me at all. That was quite a little while ago. I was only a small boy then. Anderson's daughter married a Captain Hays, a fine, big, military-looking man, and they kept on with the hotel after him. It was on the upper side of Beaver Road, just an old-fashioned country tavern, a two story brick. They used to hold the township elections there. Ohio township ran from Big Sewickley up to Jack's Run and three miles back in the country. Then there was the stone tavern at the foot of Park's Hollow (Glen Mitchell), kept by James Park; I knew Jim first rate. The road took a bend there and ran in around where the tavern stood. It has been straightened out since. Park had three sons, Jim, Jack and Wash, and he had two daughters, one, Esther, married Rudisill; the other was named Polly, I think. The old Beer tavern on the river bank was before my time.

WAY'S TAVERN, BELOW SAND HILL

"The first hotel in the village stood about where Myers's store is now, and Ague's before it. It was a frame building, two stories, and pretty close to the sidewalk. It was kept by a man named Weimer and after him by different people. Then came Little's tavern on the other side of Beaver down at the corner of Little Street, a pretty big two story frame house. It was the biggest of all the taverns. The road widened out there to fifty feet or more and the hotel stood back from the street. The stage coaches would turn in and drive up to the front door. I don't know how many people it accommodated. There was quite a big stable on the other side of Little Street where the Community Kitchen now is, with a horse trough in front of it. John Little was the proprietor. He had three sons, John, Tom and Sam.

"Across from Little's and a short way further down the road was Fife's tavern, kept by John Fife. It was a brick building of two stories, standing back from the street some and was afterwards the Academy; it burned down and was re-built, later. There was a stable just back of it.

"Down below Sand Hill was Way's tavern in the brick house, one of the oldest houses here. Old Squire John Way built it, long before my time (1810). The last Way that kept it was Nicholas who kept tavern there for awhile in my earliest recollection. Several people ran it after Way quit. The next after him was a man named Barnes; the last one was John Oliver, no relation to the Sewickley Olivers. He afterwards moved to Allegheny, on the Common.

"Next below Way's was the old stone tavern down by Little Sewickley Creek they call Lark Inn now. I think Daniel Leet built it. According to my first recollections it was kept by a man named John Might. He died there. It was called The Half Way House; half way between Pittsburgh and Beaver. There was a big sign in front of it, "Half Way House," and the name of the proprietor painted below. Robert Routh, an Englishman, followed Might; then Benjamin Pyle, a Quaker from Columbiana, Ohio; then Samuel Ritchey, Pyle's son-in-law, and he kept it as long as it was a hotel, along into the

'50's. He was keeping tavern when I came back from California."

"Captain," he was asked, "How do you account for the great number of taverns?"

"That was because there was immense traffic along the road. Great strings of wagons, Conestogas, with six-horse teams coming in from Ohio and Indiana and going to Philadelphia, I guess. Big, fine horses, with bells on them. And there would be droves of cattle, and pigs, and turkeys too. The hogs were the hardest to drive and the turkeys the easiest. Men would run along beside them with a piece of red flannel on a long pole and scare them so they would crowd together and run. They would drive easier than cattle but when it began to get dark you couldn't drive them. They would fly up into the trees and roost. I have seen the fence tops all along the road for miles covered with turkeys roosting.

"Did the taverns have large stables to accommodate the teams?"

"No, the stables weren't very big. The horses were mostly fed from the back of the wagon. The drivers carried their feed with them or bought it at the hotels. At night they would cover the horses with blankets if it was cold. The horses didn't lie down, they just stood by the wagons and slept. You would see six or eight covered wagons at the hotels in the evenings with the horses unhitched for the night. The drivers paid twelve and a half cents for their meals and would sleep on the bar-room floor, wrapped in their blankets. Every tavern had its bar; they served all kinds of liquors, brandy, beer, etc., but whisky was the main drink. A drink of whisky cost three cents, two for a nickel, so you could treat a man for a nickel, but they didn't have nickels then, just the little silver five cent pieces. Old Captain Hays kept two brands of whisky, one at five cents a glass and the other at ten cents. He would ask you which you wanted—and they were all the same, came out of the same barrel."

THE HALF WAY HOUSE, NOW "LARK INN"

"Were there stage coaches on the road too?"

"Yes, there was a stage coach every day, one each way. The only post office between Pittsburgh and Beaver was at Mr. Shields's house, where Mrs. Williams lives now. Sewickley Bottom it was. The stage stopped mostly at Might's Half Way House, but sometimes at Little's, and at Way's, too, depending on the best terms they could get; for so many horses, so many passengers. The passengers would get their meals while the horses were changed. There would be maybe six or eight passengers in the coach and there were right comfortable rooms for them if they stopped over, but generally they kept right on, slept in the coach, for it didn't stop over night. The stage coach carried mail and would drive in and out at Mr. Shields's to change the mail. Mr. Shields sometimes would go to Philadelphia on horseback and stop every night at one of his hotels; he owned a chain of taverns. He wouldn't be very long gone, either.

"I guess that is about all that I remember about the old taverns along the road. There were many of them and they were busy places with the heavy traffic of those days."

August, 1928.

EARLY SEWICKLEY

EARLY SEWICKLEY

FURTHER REMINISCENCES OF CAPTAIN ANDERSON

Captain Anderson's chats about old times, whether recounting the colorful experiences of an exceptionally long and eventful life or merely recalling early days in the Sewickley Valley, had a flavor all their own. A lively sense of humor, a cheerful philosophy and a marvelously clear memory were his and to draw him out in conversation was a delight. The following notes give merely the substance of one of his talks; much of their charm evaporates in reducing his reminiscences to writing.

* * * *

Asked about the general appearance of Sewickley as he first knew it, Captain Anderson said:

"Well, there weren't but a few stores along the street, mostly vacant lots. At the corner of Broad and Beaver streets, where the Peoples Bank is, old Robert Green had a general store. It was the same building that Sylvester Ritchey kept store in before the bank, and part of it is there yet. Then, Mrs. John Garrison had a little store down where the picture house now is. Just a little store it was, where she sold cider, candy, ginger cakes and tobacco.

"John Garrison made bricks and had his brickyard about where Ben Campney's stable is, across from Mrs. Garrison's store. That is Locust Place now. Quite a street. We used to call it "Coffee Pot Alley." Garrison used steers, oxen, to tramp the mud for the bricks. I used to watch them when I was a boy. It was Garrison that built the house on Hopkins Street where Mrs. Gormly lived. He lived part of the time over the store.

THE VILLAGE OF SEWICKLEY

"His two boys went to school where I did, in the little brick schoolhouse that Mr. Shields built on the hill above Beaver Road. The first teacher I went to was named Peacock. After he went away William Reno taught, father of Elias Reno; then John Way. He used to keep store at the corner of Beaver and Chestnut. Gaston's it was afterwards, now Watson's. They called him John Senior. He was a cousin of John Way, Jr. The teachers were paid by the patrons, by subscription. That was before the free schools. I suppose thirty-five or forty children attended. It was all Ohio Township then, before they struck off Sewickley. At Christmas time we used to bar the teacher out and wouldn't let him in till he would sign a paper for a treat, and we would bring it up to Mrs. Garrison's store and get cider and gingerbread and apples for Christmas. They'd all go pretty good right now, wouldn't they?

"There was a little half-way kind of a store next to Weimer's tavern, about where Hegner's now is, but Bob Green's was the principal store and there wasn't much else

MRS. GARRISON'S STORE

THE LITTLE BRICK SCHOOL HOUSE

but open lots. It wasn't much of a place. They called it 'Fifetown' after John Fife who kept the tavern; had called it 'Dogtown' and down on the river where the Hoeys lived, they called it 'Hoey's Point.' I remember it was called "Oppotongo" too; Indian name, I guess; but the people wouldn't stand for that and named it Sewickleyville. Right up here where I live (Centennial, east of Broad Street) it was all in big oak timber; hadn't been cleared out yet; it all belonged to Samuel Peebles who bought out the Beer family and moved into the Beer house. His brother Robert built further up, toward the hill, the frame house afterwards the home of Robert H. Davis.

"And I remember the chestnut grove down where the railroad now is. This was all covered with trees about here. You turned off the road at McElwain's corner (Beaver and Division Streets) and went right through woods down to the graveyard. You know where that was. The High School is there now.

"There wasn't much of anything on Beaver Street east of Division Street; just open lots. That all belonged to Dr. Hopkins; he bought it from the Peebles. The little store kept by James Porter and his wife came along later. It stood a little bit east of Chestnut Street.

"Across from Little's tavern on Beaver Street, where the Baptist Church is, was a vacant lot where Dr. John Dickson built his home. Old Dr. Dickson was a great surgeon and practiced in Pittsburgh before he came down here. I remember him very well. He was one of a lot of witnesses that were subpoenaed to testify to the value of land in the McKean tract, 2400 acres, eight farms of 300 acres each, where the Country Club is and all those homes. I was subpoenaed with the rest and so was my brother Dave. Wade Hampton, the lawyer in charge of the proceedings, called on Dr. Dickson first and asked him if he knew the McKean tract, was familiar with it. 'Yes,' said the doctor, 'I know it well. I have practiced medicine over it in the daytime and hunted 'coons over it at night and it is worth $8.00 an acre.' 'Why,' said Mr. Hampton, 'the timber on it is worth more than that.' 'No, it isn't,' said Dr. Dickson, 'Old John McPherson cut the best timber off it to make kegs and Jim Brooks made baskets of the younger timber. It all went long ago.' And he stuck to his story. Eight dollars. I was called next and added two dollars, said it was worth ten dollars an acre. You couldn't buy it for that now."

"When did you come to Sewickley to live, Captain?"

"When I was married, in 1857. I was on the river then. I bought the house on Beaver Street where I lived for eight years, when I sold it to William Stoops, 1865. The lot fronted sixty feet on Beaver Street and ran clear back to what is now Centennial. The brick house on the lot was built by Jock

Dickson, brother of Robert Dickson. His name was John but we called him 'Jock' as he was a kind of a horse jockey. The place had passed out of his hands to David Shields, grandfather of Captain Dave, and from him to John Thompson who sold it to me. Dr. Chantler was pretty nearly the last one to live in it; it was torn down a few years ago and a new building put up where George McDonald lives, No. 537 Beaver Street.

"Next door to me, as you go towards Broad Street, was another brick house that old William Miller built, we called him 'Billie' Miller, father of John Miller who keeps the shoe store. The year after I moved in he built the story and a half brick house at the corner of Broad and Hill and moved up there. He rented the house next to me to Dr. Alex. Black, father of Mrs. Snyder and Mrs. Adair and Sam Black, the real estate man. There was a big family of them and I knew them all well; neighbors to me for seven years. The Blacks lived there till 1864, then they moved to their house on Wylie Street in Pittsburgh.

"Next to Dr. Black was old Dr. William Woods, father of Charlie Woods who afterwards ran the drug store at the corner of Broad and Beaver. Dr. Woods was a tall fine-looking old man and wore a long white beard. There was an 'upping block' in front of his house, a white oak stump with a step sawed into it so that the women who came to see the Doctor could get on and off their horses. Next to Dr. Woods was the brick house and store of Squire George H. Starr, and it's there yet, directly opposite the end of Division Street. Squire Starr and his wife kept the store. She was a Miss Hooker, one of the teachers in the Edgeworth Seminary. Mrs. Olver (not Oliver, *Olver*) brought her and another teacher, Miss Johnston, with her when she moved her school here from Braddock. They were both pretty well up in years but they got married. Miss Johnston married old Jimmie Olver after Mrs. Olver died. They were married in the Daniel Nevin house in Edgeworth and lived there; Daniel Nevin moved over to the Seminary and ran it.—Did you know how Mrs. Olver happened to move her school down here?

"Susan and Hannah Shields, two of David Shields's daughters, went to the Seminary while it was in Braddock and Mrs. Olver visited them at their home down by Little Sewickley Creek. She liked the place so much she moved her school here. Susan married Isaac Cook, Mrs. Martha Williams's father (Mrs. L. Halsey Williams). I knew him well. He was a preacher down at Beaver and followed Rev. Andrew B. Quay, father of Senator Matthew Stanley Quay. Hannah never married. Eliza was the oldest; she married John K. Wilson; then there was Rebecca; she never married either.

"The house next to me, to the east, was of brick too. Mrs. Rinehart lived there; widow of Squire Rinehart, an alderman in Pittsburgh. The house is still there, next to the A. & P. store. Her son Joe married Lizzie Allison, daughter of Dr. Allison and his first wife, my sister Mary. Joe was a railroad man, afterwards was president of the Santa Fé railroad. The next house, brick too, was James Ellis's, and on the corner of Straight street John McLaughlin's, where Wat Marlatt lives. Mrs. Nicols, who lived there, was a daughter of John McLaughlin.

"All of that row of houses were brick. Squire Starr's stood near the street, for it was a store. All of the rest stood back a piece and there was a fence all along in front with gates; pretty nice looking street. On the other side was Rev. Andrew Black who lived in the brick house still standing at the corner of Logan Street. I don't know who built it. Yes, I used to hear Logan called 'Snuffgulligan' but I don't know where they got that name. Andrew Black was Dr. Alex. Black's brother, a Methodist preacher but he had to quit preaching on account of his chest. His wife was a Roseburg, daughter of Captain Roseburg who lived where the E. B. Taylor family now lives, at Roseburg Station, that was just above Quaker Valley. Mrs. Andrew Black, or Mrs. Martha Black as she was called when she was a widow, built the big frame house on Beaver Street below Grant Street that was afterwards the Bevington House. It was burned down. She was a temperance reformer and that was long before prohibition. She and her son Wat used to march around trying to close up saloons, breaking bottles, etc. Her daughter Mary married Dr. Woods's oldest son Will. He died and left her with two boys, Billy and Wat who died young. Dr. Woods's other son, Charles, married Col. McKelvy's daughter Julia.

"There were some brick houses on Beaver Street, across from the row I lived in, built before I came there. A double house just across from me; Squire Rudisill lived in one end of it. And a brick house on each side of it. The one next to Watson's store is still there. It was rented to different families. Dr. McCready's brother, a Methodist preacher, was living there when I came.

"Then on the corner of Chestnut Street was the frame house and store built by John Way, Sr., cousin of John Way, Jr. He lived there and kept store. One of his daughters married Sam Gaston and it was Gaston's store later; now it's Watson's. Across Chestnut from this was a frame house where four Miller boys lived; all carpenters; no relation to the other Millers. When they widened Chestnut this house was moved back to Washington Street.

"I guess that is about all I can tell you about Beaver Street when I lived there."

August, 1928.

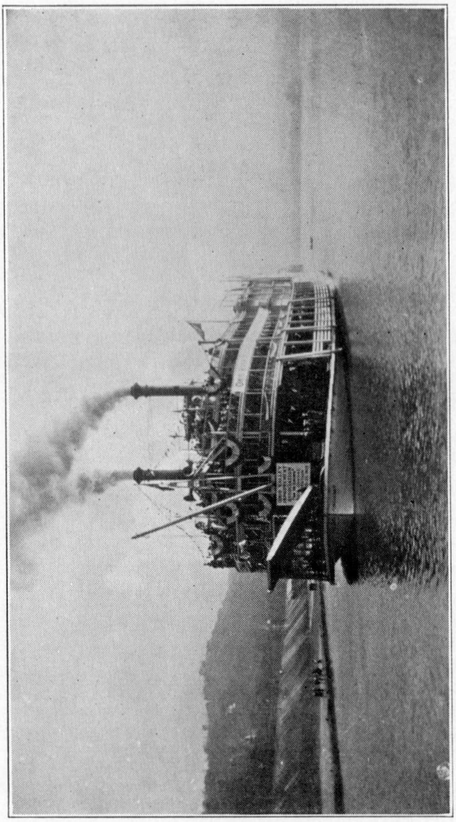

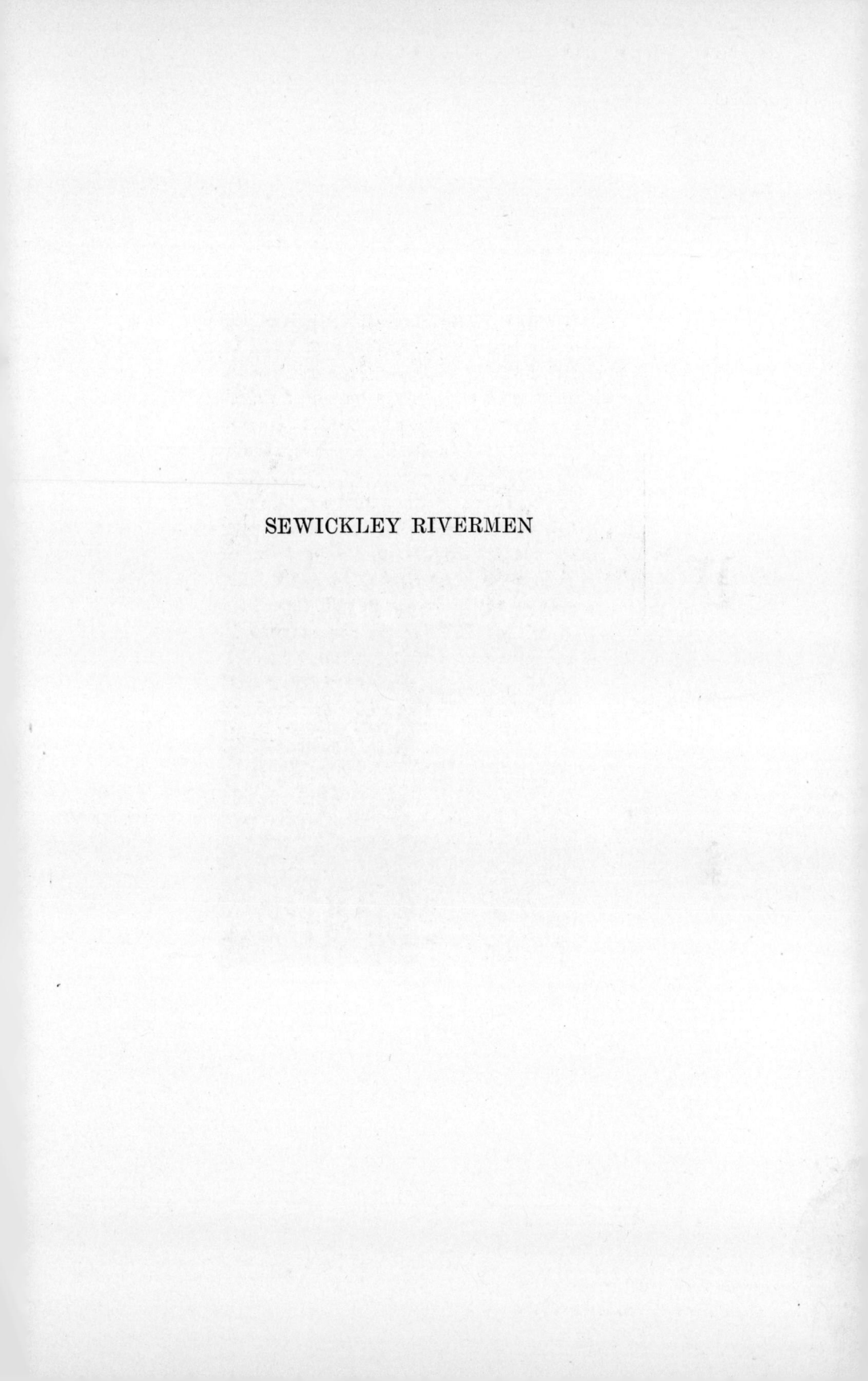

SEWICKLEY RIVERMEN

THE "DICK FULTON" PILOT HOUSE
Now overlooks the river from Captain Fred Dippold's former home

SEWICKLEY RIVERMEN

AS REMEMBERED BY CAPTAIN ANDERSON

SEWICKLEY has long been favored as the home of railroad men, both high officials and employees. There was a time when it was equally popular with rivermen—steamboat captains, pilots and mates. Captain John C. Anderson in a recent chat about the river drew on his memories of past years and, in substance, related the following:

"There used to be a lot of steamboat captains and river pilots living in and about Sewickley. Going back to my earliest recollections, there was Jim Smith. He lived down at Deadman's Island and we called him 'Deadman Jim Smith'; a well-known pilot; pretty rough he was, the bully of the river. He married Polly Bean, a granddaughter of Major Leet. Her mother was Polly, too, Polly Leet, before she married Bean. She was a sister of Eliza Leet who married Mr. Shields. Jim Smith and Jim Park, who kept the tavern up at Park's Hollow, were the only ones who ever called Mr. Shields by his first name. Jim Smith would come into the post office at Sewickley Bottom—Mr. Shields was the postmaster there—and call out, "Hello, Uncle Dave!" He built the one-story stone house that stood on what is now the corner of Academy and Beaver Street. He lived and died there. I just don't remember when he built it. Little "Davy," the dwarf, lived in it afterwards—I suppose you remember him?

"There were four McDonalds, all pilots and captains. The oldest, John V. McDonald, lived at Beaver; Dave McDonald came next. He married Dr. Woods's daughter Mary. His first wife was a Dowds. Then there was Marshall McDonald, generally called "Marsh." He lived at the upper end of the borough in what is now Glen Osborne (the Henry W. Davis house, now the home of Horace F. Baker.—F. T. N.). And last, there was Joe McDonald, all four pilots and captains and their father, John McDonald, was a pilot before them. He lived opposite Economy. The fifth son, J. Sharp McDonald, wasn't a river man. The McDonald boats, I don't remember their names, were tow-boats; carried coal from Pittsburgh to Louisville. Fred Dippold, a captain and pilot, lived on the river bank up by Glen Osborne. His tow-boat *Tigress* belonged to his father, John Dippold. Fred was a good pilot and knew the river. David Gilmore, I knew him well. You remember where he lived, down by the railroad (now the site of the High School.—F. T. N.). He was captain of a packet in the Pittsburgh-Cincinnati trade; what was known as "transient" trade; go anywhere—sometimes to St. Louis, sometimes to New Orleans. George W. Cochran who lived next to Captain Gilmore (now the home of Don Rose, Esq.) was first a clerk with his brother Robert and later rose to be captain. He ran on packet boats, too. I don't recall their names. Jehu P. Smith was another pilot and captain. He lived on Bank Street, corner of Graham. He was a tow-boat man. William Stoops who bought my house on Beaver Street in 1865 was captain of several boats at different times; carried both passengers and freight to St. Louis, sometimes to New Orleans. His last boat was the *J. S. Pringle*, the one I told you of that had double engines and two stern wheels. She could stop and turn right around on herself. Captain William Cunningham I didn't know. He was Captain George Cunningham's father, a tow-boat captain. James Porter was another. First clerk, then captain of the *Argosy*, a packet in the transient trade; ran anywhere. That was before the war. He first clerked with Robert Cochran, Captain George Cochran's brother.

"James Logan and George Rowley were two fine pilots but they didn't live here. Mr. Logan was Mrs. Fred Dippold's father. They vouched for me when I went up to get my pilot's license. I got it in three years because I studied the river. I was very ambitious to be a pilot and I worked and studied the river when some of the other young fellows just had a good time. I'll admit that I had special opportunities. I would run with Mr. Logan and handle the boat on his watch under his direction. He'd let me take her down the riffles and make landings; so I got my license in three years. There were no lights then to steer by. You depended on the lead. Two leadsmen stood near the bow, one to the starboard, one to port. They'd sing out 'Six feet,' 'Seven feet,' like that, and at ten feet, 'Mark twain.' Then if it got over ten feet 'Mark under water twain;' 'Mark three' was twelve feet. This was all below Louisville. Didn't use the leads above that. The leadsmen could tell the depth at night by the feel of the leads as well as by day. 'Mark Twain'—that's the name Clemens took for his writings. I met Clemens several times, but I didn't know him well. He learned the river under old Bixby, a Mississippi river pilot. Clemens says to him after making a landing, 'How do you know where to land in the dark? I can't see any landing.' Bixby says, 'I'll make a pilot out of ye or I'll kill ye.'

"The sand bars shifted all the time. When the leadsman would call 'Five feet'—'Four feet,' etc., then you'd stop her and back out. 'That's not the channel!' You learned to know the landmarks on shore. Coming down from Pittsburgh there was Merriman's Riffle, below Lowrie's Run. When you got directly opposite the white church on Neville Island you pulled her sharp over to the south bank. That's where the channel was. Pilots could see that church at night, if nobody else could. Then when you could see light through a gap in the hills on the right bank you steered through White's Riffle and so down through the Trap (opposite Glen Osborne station). That's the way you had to know the river.

"I used to work on the farm at my home in Leetsdale— the house is still there. Riter & Conley own it now—or did. I saw the towboats and packets go by and wished that some day I could be a pilot. Then when the gold excitement broke out, I went to California—in 1849. When I came back in 1851 my mother asked Captain Sam Young to give me a job on one of his boats to keep me from going back to the gold mines. He had built the *J. M. Harris,* named for Captain Harris (he married a Shouse). Captain Young sold me an interest in her that I paid for with money I'd brought back from California and I shipped with her as second mate. That was my first boat. Afterwards I was first mate. She ran up the Chattahoochee river carrying cotton to New Orleans; there she loaded up with sugar for Pittsburgh and would lie up at Shousetown for the winter. We sold her down in Arkansas. My second boat was the *Alliance;* I was part owner and mate on her. After one year we sold her, too, and Captain Young built the *Rescue.* I had an interest in her and in a lot of boats after her. I don't remember all of their names. It was on the *Rescue* that I learned to pilot, steering her under Mr. Logan's direction during his watch. We sold her after one season. Captain Young's next boat was the *Challenge.* That was the packet with the double engines and double paddle wheels. I piloted her. Then came the *Progress* and the *Reliance*, both packets in the transient trade—Cincinnati, Nashville, St. Louis. Then the *Undine,* Captain John Woodburn. He lived in Edgeworth. His two brothers were steamboat captains, too. Jim built the house in Beaver Street (No. 322 Beaver) where he lived. Ben lived in Shousetown. I'll tell you about Ben. He had made his pile at steamboating, made a lot of money, then he quit and went to studying to be a preacher. From steamboating to preaching! He studied for a United Presbyterian but when he got through they said to him, 'You're more of a Baptist than a U. P.' So he turned Baptist and preached in the old Baptist Church on Sandusky Street, Allegheny, till he died. After the *Undine* came the *Kenton.* Maybe the *H. H. Conn* was before that. I had a part interest in all the boats Captain Young built beginning with the *J. M. Harris.* The *J. H. Conn* was named after a steamboat agent at St. Louis, a packet. She was burned afterwards at the Pittsburgh wharf in 1858. Those that had steam up backed out in the stream; the rest were burned up.

"I had an interest in a lot of boats afterwards. In war time I was captain and pilot on the Cumberland river. Ran the *Alpha;* had an interest in her, too. We sold her to the government. Quartermaster Stevens bought her at Nashville. We were carrying stuff for Sherman's army, from March to

August, 1864, everything; soldiers, horses, cattle and fixed ammunition. We were mighty glad when we got all that ammunition unloaded! We took on stuff at Smith's Landing, sixty miles above Cairo and carried it two hundred miles to Nashville; that was a military post. Then there was the *Kate B. Porter,* in war time; Captain Joe Porter, son of Ezra Porter of Shousetown. I went as her pilot the first trip, Pittsburgh to Nashville. From there they sent me to Burnside's Point, 470 miles above Nashville on the Cumberland river. Burnside's Point was being evacuated by the Union troops. They took out everything, carried away what they could and burned the rest, then marched the soldiers off to join Sherman. We were 435 miles outside the Union lines. That was when we had boiler iron around the place where the pilot stood to protect against bullets. We had a gunboat along to make it safe. Burnside's Point is on the south fork of the Cumberland river and to get there we went out of Tennessee through Kentucky and into Virginia.

"After this I was on the *Glide,* built by my brother William, who lived in Shousetown. We sold her to the government and built *Glide No. 2* and *Glide No. 3*; she was sunk in the Red River. Then came the *R. C. Gray,* named for Captain Gray. That was after the war was over. I had an interest in the *Ezra Porter,* too; built by Captain Joe Porter and named for his father. We lost a lot of money on that boat. That's all I can remember the names of just now. Maybe some more will come to me. There were Captain Sam Young's boats, and Ezra's—Ezra Young is my nephew. The river was a busy life in those days, and Shousetown and Sewickley saw a lot of it.

September, 1928.

* * * *

One week after the date of this interview Captain Anderson died, October 6, 1928, aged one hundred years, eight months and twenty-two days. It was intended that he should check up certain names and dates in the first draft of this paper, but the opportunity slipped by and was lost.

SEWICKLEY RAILROAD MEN

GEN. GEORGE W. CASS

SEWICKLEY RAILROAD MEN

SOME HIGH OFFICIALS WHO ONCE LIVED HERE

The Ohio and Pennsylvania Railroad Company was incorporated by acts of the Ohio and Pennsylvania legislatures, passed the 24th February and 11th April, 1848, by which, and by an Act of Assembly of Pennsylvania, passed 14th December, 1854, this road was to be connected with the Pennsylvania Railroad in the city of Pittsburgh by a bridge across the Allegheny river. It ran its first passenger train through Sewickleyville on July 4th, 1851, a gala day in the Valley. On August 1st, 1856, there was effected a consolidation with the Ohio and Indiana and the Fort Wayne and Chicago Railroad, the three lines jointly connecting Pittsburgh and Chicago. This consolidated line was named the Pittsburgh, Fort Wayne and Chicago Railroad. This company became financially involved and the road was sold under foreclosure on October 24, 1861, to agents of a new company which was formed February 26, 1862, under the name Pittsburgh, Fort Wayne and Chicago Railway Company.

In 1890 the western lines centering in Pittsburgh were absorbed by the Pennsylvania Railroad and were designated the "Pennsylvania Lines West." Since 1920, when these railroads came back from Federal administration, which had been in effect during the World War, they have been incorporated in the Pennsylvania System, of which they now constitute the Central Division.

From the earliest days of the railroad's history Sewickley has been the place of residence chosen by many of its officials, in fact, a very remarkable number have lived here in the past and there are today as many as ten or more prominent railroad men who make the Sewickley valley their home. Limiting this historical foot-note to the past, and making mention only of those officials who formerly lived here, we go back to George W. Cass, who heads the list.

General Cass was born in Muskingum County, Ohio, in 1810. He lived for some years in Detroit as a member of the family of his uncle, General Lewis Cass, who was successively Secretary of War in President Jackson's cabinet, United States Senator from Michigan, Secretary of State under Buchanan and United States envoy to France. George W. Cass was graduated from West Point in 1832 with high honors but resigned the service in 1836 to take up the engineering profession. He became actively interested in the Adams Express Company and in 1854 was elected president of all the consolidated Adams Express lines between Boston and St. Louis. In 1856 he was living in Brownsville, Pa., and in that year he removed to Pittsburgh where he was elected president of the Ohio and Pennsylvania Railroad, succeeding General William Robinson of Allegheny. He was, in the same year, made the first president of the consolidated Pittsburgh, Fort Wayne and Chicago Railroad (afterwards "Railway") and held the position until 1881, when he resigned the office but continued as director and trustee down to the time of his death. In 1867 he became largely interested in the Northern Pacific Railroad and in 1872 he succeeded to its presidency. In 1875 the Federal court appointed him receiver of the road. After resigning the presidency of the "Fort Wayne" he retired from active railroading and spent his latter years in New York City, where he was senior warden of Christ's Church, and where he died March 21, 1888.

It is the period between 1863 and 1873 that especially interests us, for it was then that he lived in what is now the borough of Osborn. He and his wife bought land in Ohio township, as it was then called, adjoining property of Judge Warner, lying on both sides of the Beaver Road and extending down to the railroad. Here General Cass built a large and beautiful mansion which he named "Cassella," a composite of his wife's name and his own. With its lovely garden, its orchard and vineyard, its graded grass-covered slopes and stately forest trees, it was by far the most beautiful and attractive home in the Valley. This house in recent years was the Sewickley home of Mrs. Mary Roberts Rinehart. Here Mr. and Mrs. Cass lived until 1873 and here their daughter Sophia L. Cass was married to Francis M. Hutchinson in the year 1866. Mr. Hutchinson had entered the service of the Pittsburgh, Fort Wayne and Chicago in 1862, and in 1865 he was appointed Secretary and Treasurer, which positions he held until his death, which occurred in 1882. He lived in Sewickley throughout his married life, first in a brick house on Chestnut Street that formerly stood next to the John McMillen house, and from December, 1866, in the house at the corner of Broad and Frederick where, it is a pleasure to note, Mrs. Hutchinson still lives; the house to which she came so soon after her marriage.

James D. Layng served as Assistant General Superintendent under J. N. McCullough, General Superintendent, during the presidency of General Cass. Later he became General Manager of the Pittsburgh, Fort Wayne and Chicago Railway, holding that position until 1881. He came from Steubenville, Ohio, in 1873 and took up his residence on the terrace fronting upon the railroad, at Edgeworth. With him came his brother-in-law, Basil W. Doyle, as his assistant, who also was long a resident of Edgeworth and Sewickley. In 1881 Mr. Layng went to Chicago where he was made General Manager of the Chicago and Northwestern, Mr. Doyle going with him as Secretary. In 1884 he removed to New York where he became president of the West Shore railroad and a member of the Vanderbilt Board. During his connection with the "Fort Wayne," as its General Manager, George S. Griscom, also an Edgeworth resident, was Superintendent of the Pittsburgh Division, in which position he was followed by Arthur B. Starr, whose home was on Linden and later on Academy Avenue.

Mr. Layng's successor as General Manager was William A. Baldwin, who came here from Williamsport, Pa., in 1881, making his home at the corner of Shields and Nursery Lanes in the house which later was the residence of Mr. J. J. Brooks. Here he lived until 1888 when he removed to Rochester, N. Y., where he was connected with the Buffalo, Rochester and Pittsburgh Railroad until 1900. In that year he returned to Pittsburgh to accept the presidency of the Cleveland and Marietta R. R. which office he held until 1905, when he was retired. From 1900 until his death in 1911 he lived on Maple Lane, Sewickley.

Following Mr. Baldwin as General Manager of the "Fort Wayne," came Leonor F. Loree, who is today perhaps the most prominent railroad man in the United States. To enumerate the various offices that he has held, even to list all that he occupies today, would unduly prolong the present paper. Suffice it to say that he is now President and Chairman of the Executive Committee of the Delaware and Hudson Company, also president and director of thirty-four companies controlled by or affiliated with it. He has recently been much in the public eye by reason of his efforts to secure control of a number of roads whereby another route would be opened from the West into the metropolitan area and a powerful competitor created for the New York Central and the Pennsylvania systems. During the World War he held high governmental posts. Mr. Loree while with the Pittsburgh, Fort Wayne and Chicago as General Manager lived at Shields, on the terrace overlooking the railroad, in the house which later was the home of Mrs. Agnes Graff. From there he moved to the former A. B. Starr house on Linden Avenue, next to the Frank Semple residence.

Joseph W. Rinehart, a brother of C. Stanley Rinehart, the artist, several of whose paintings hang in the permanent collection of the Carnegie Art Gallery, was another Sewickley railroad man who went far in his chosen career. He began as a car checker in the Allegheny Valley railroad yards; later rose to be Auditor, then, after a period with the Baltimore & Ohio Railroad, he secured a position with the Santa Fé railroad and in the 'Nineties became its president. His first Sewickley home was on Beaver Street, about opposite the end of Chestnut, where he lived with his mother, the widow of 'Squire Rinehart, a Pittsburgh alderman. Joseph Rinehart married Elizabeth Allison, daughter of Rev. James Allison and Mary Allison, his first wife, who was a sister of Captain John C. Anderson. Mr. and Mrs. Rinehart made their home at the corner of Walnut and Elwick Streets. If you had asked any Sewickley boy in the late 'Seventies or the 'Eighties about "Joe" Rinehart you would have learned that he was famed as a baseball player, and especially known as an immaculate dresser. Whether in street clothes or in hunting costume he was always sartorially correct.

Sidney B. Liggett in 1871 was a clerk in the office of the Auditor of the Pittsburgh, Fort Wayne and Chicago Railway. In 1879 he became Assistant Secretary, and in 1881 Secretary of the Pennsylvania Lines West, which position he held until his death in 1915. In 1877 he came to Sewickley and made his home on Chestnut Street below Thorn.

As Signal Engineer of the Lines West, William McC. Grafton served for many years down to the time of his death which occurred in 1913. He lived on Beaver Street below Blackburn, later removing to the former Dr. Allison residence at the southwest corner of Beaver and Academy Avenue.

H. L. Howard Blair, Assistant General Manager of the Lines West, was a life-long resident of the Valley, living on Bank Street near Little. Mr. Blair died in 1928.

Charles Watts, whose home fronted on the railroad near Edgeworth station, was General Superintendent of Passenger Transportation. J. C. Bland, Chief Engineer of Bridge and Buildings, lived on Thorn Street and, later, in Edgeworth. Upon his retirement in 1923 he was succeeded by James F. Leonard, son-in-law of Robert Trimble. Their home overlooks the recently abandoned site of Glen Osborne station. Mr. Trimble was retired only a few months ago as Chief Engineer of the Pennsylvania lines west of Pittsburgh and, since 1920, Assistant Chief Engineer of the entire Pennsylvania System.

J. Morton Hall, who lived at the corner of Bank and Walnut Streets, in the house which is now the residence of Mrs. Melchior Chaplin, was General Passenger Agent of the Allegheny Valley Railroad, and afterwards Assistant to Vice President King of the Baltimore and Ohio. He died more than twenty years ago.

Mr. Charles B. Price, brother-in-law of Mrs. Edward A. Woods, was also for many years connected with the Allegheny Valley, first as Superintendent of the Pittsburgh Division, later as General Manager of the road, which position he resigned in

1902. For over twenty years he lived in Sewickley; his death occurred in 1923.

Rudolf Lipp had a long career as a railroad man, his position upon retirement being that of Assistant to the General Passenger Agent, Pennsylvania Lines. He and his wife, who is a daughter of Rev. Robert Hopkins, Sewickley's first burgess, live at No. 316 Broad Street. Sewickley has been their home for more years than it is possible to state.

George L. Potter, who formerly lived at the corner of Nevin Avenue and Beaver Street, was, while a resident here, General Manager of the Pennsylvania Lines. About 1901 he moved to Baltimore, where he held the office of Vice President of the Baltimore and Ohio Railroad. He died about five years ago.

Dr. Samuel C. Scott, Assistant to the President of the Pennsylvania Railroad, lived on Thorn Street below Grant, for many years a respected member of our community. Two officials of the P. C. C. & St. L. Railway will be readily recalled to memory: John H. Dury, Paymaster, whose home was on Maple Lane, and Michael C. Spencer, Cashier of that road, who lived on Walnut Street below the Fort Wayne tracks.

J. Judson Brooks, who succeeded his brother J. Twing Brooks as General Counsel for the Pittsburgh, Fort Wayne and Chicago Railway, and later for the Lines West, lived at the corner of Shields and Nursery Lanes. Upon his death, in 1914, he was succeeded by Judge C. B. Heiserman, who came from Urbana, Ohio, where he was on the Circuit Court bench. It was with regret that we saw him transferred to Philadelphia, in 1921, although he was to be congratulated upon his rise to the office of Vice President in charge of Legal Affairs. His home while a resident here was for a time in the building which is now the Dorian Club, on Broad Street, and later on Linden Place.

Of Vice Presidents it would appear that Sewickley has had more than a fair share. There was Edward B. Taylor, Second Vice President in charge of Finance, whose home on Linden Avenue overlooks the railroad at what, in the old days, was Roseburg station. Mr. Taylor was one of our foremost citizens; public spirited, highly esteemed. He will long be remembered especially for his enthusiastic interest in the borough water system, as head of the Water Commission. He died November 8th, 1922.

D. T. McCabe, who retired a few years ago and now lives in Atlantic City, was Fourth Vice President in charge of Traffic of the Lines West. His home was for many years on Thorn Street at the corner of Little, now the Nelson Van Kleeck residence.

T. H. B. McKnight upon his retirement this year had completed more than fifty years in the service, rising from the position of messenger to that of Treasurer of the Lines West, and since 1920, Treasurer of the Central, Northwestern and Southwestern Regions of the Pennsylvania System, of which the Pennsylvania lines west of Pittsburgh are now a part. Altogether, he held the position of Treasurer for thirty-eight years and, a short time before the end of his service, he was promoted to the Vice Presidency of the Pennsylvania Company and of the Pittsburgh, Cincinnati, Chicago and St. Louis Railway. Mr McKnight was a lifelong resident of Sewickley. His home was for many years on Thorn Street below Grant and, more recently, on Centennial Avenue, at Pine Road. He has within the past few months moved to Washington, D. C.

George L. Peck, Fifth Vice President of the Lines West, and later, Vice President in charge of Personnel, with headquarters in Philadelphia, was one of our valued citizens and an elder in the Presbyterian church. His home until 1920 was in Sewickley.

Of our younger men who have made their mark in railroad circles, and, in the course of promotion have been lost to Sewickley, W. Miller Wardrop, son of Mr. Robert Wardrop, has had perhaps the most noteworthy career. Rising through successive promotions he has recently been transferred from Wilmington, Delaware, where he was General Superintendent of the Southern Division, to Detroit where he now holds the position of Assistant Vice President.

Charles H. Matthews when living on Thorn Street, below Grant, was General Passenger Agent. Recently he was transferred to Philadelphia and made General Traffic Manager in charge of Passenger Traffic and has been one of the prime movers in the Pennsylvania Railroad's aviation branch, the Transcontinental Air Transport, Inc.

Two Sewickley boys who progressed side by side in the railroad service should be mentioned, A. Howard Shaw and C. Curtis Blair. The former is now in New York City as General Traffic Manager, while the latter when he resigned a few years ago, was Assistant Treasurer of the Western Region, with offices in Chicago.

While the scope of the present paper was to be limited to officials now deceased, or who have removed from the Valley, an exception was made in referring to Robert Trimble, who is retired but still lives with us. This sketchy article should not end without another infraction of the rule, in mention of John J. Koch, Assistant to the General Traffic Manager of the Pennsylvania Railroad System, who completed his fiftieth year of railroad service within the present year. Mr. Koch, a valued citizen of our borough, has long made his home on Thorn Street west of Little.

To include a biographical note concerning each of the ten or a dozen officials who now live in Sewickley; to follow this with mere mention of the twenty or more who lived here but a short time and were transferred elsewhere; to add to these a list of the numerous holders of minor positions, would be to extend this paper beyond reasonable limits.

Glance back over this partial catalogue of men high in the service of the Pennsylvania Railroad and of its earlier constituent companies, and you must be impressed with the fact that since the middle of the last century Sewickley has been, in a certain sense, pre-eminently a railroad town.

November, 1929.

THE PASSING OF TWO LANDMARKS

THE OSBURN HOMESTEAD

THE PASSING OF TWO LANDMARKS

A HISTORY OF THE GILMORE AND OSBURN HOUSES

IN May, 1925, ground was broken for the High School Building at the corner of Peebles and Graham Streets and the work was thereafter pushed to an early completion, in the course of which two well-known landmarks, the Gilmore and Osburn dwellings, were necessarily swept away. The history of these houses is not without interest and is worthy of preservation.

* * * *

Away back in 1825 "Judge" Griswold E. Warner, a rich lumber merchant of Olean, N. Y., came to Pittsburgh and made his home in Alleghenytown where he lived until 1858. He had served with a New York regiment in the War of 1812. Real estate seems to have been his hobby, for between the years 1831 and 1873 the records show him to have made upwards of eighty purchases of land in the county and between four hundred and five hundred sales. Among his many land ventures one especially appealed to his daughter Henrietta, who longed for a home in the country. Accordingly, in the year 1858, Judge Warner and his family moved down to Sewickley and occupied the house which he had bought in May of that year from Hon. David N. White, publisher of the Pittsburgh *Daily Gazette*, who had built it about the year 1854. This house stood in a five acre tract fronting on the railroad, extending back to Harbaugh Street and along Harbaugh Street to Graham Street. Thus it lay on both sides of the line dividing Daniel Leet's District from that of Nathaniel Breading (or Braden), two of the Deputy Surveyors who laid out the Depreciation Lands in this part of the state. That dividing line, where it passes through our borough is marked by

THE GILMORE HOUSE

Division Street, which runs due north and south (or nearly so). The portion of D. N. White's (and his wife, Dianna's), property which lay to the west of the line and in Leet's District was a bit of Section No. 1, called "Loretto," while that to the east of the line was in "Aleppo" farm, No. 126, of Braden's survey. The title to the former portion came to "Deacon" White, as he was called, from Sophia Harbaugh, a daughter of the Rev. Charles Thorn, and was a part of the original Hoey tract, while the eastern portion was deeded to White by the Rev. Robert Hopkins, having come down from the Peebles and Beer line. Back in 1810, a cholera scare had swept over Pittsburgh, and the then owners of the adjoining farms, "Aleppo" and "Loretto," set aside an acre upon their dividing line to be used as a burying ground. This one acre tract was included in the conveyance by D. N. White to Judge Warner but, as the deed recites, "only so far as he might be able to give title thereto." It was not until its abandonment as a burying ground and the removal of the bodies to the Sewickley Cemetery in 1860, that full title was vested in the owner.

It was in the summer of 1850, while visiting in Virginia, at Shannondale Springs with her brother James, that Henrietta Warner met Franklin Osburn, a young Virginian, who fell in love with and shortly thereafter married her. Coming north the young couple lived for a number of years in what is now Osborn Borough, where Judge Warner built them the house which later became the residence of James W. Arrott In the year 1868, the father set aside for his daughter one and a half acres from the eastern portion of his Sewickley property and built thereon the "Osburn" house, employing a curious pressed brick of peculiar texture and unusually large dimensions. Each window-sill was composed of a single brick, the ornate lintels made of large moulded designs, while the first course, laid upon the foundation walls, was of immense blocks with the appearance of cut stone. These bricks were made by a Sewickley company of which Charles McKnight was the head. The brickyard was located across the river at Anderson

Road, just above Shousetown. Two other buildings of this same brick are still standing in the borough; one on Broad Street, built by D. N. White and long occupied by him, is now the Dorian Club; the other, located on Pine Road, next to the J. M. Tate residence, was built by Mr. McKnight in 1866.

Judge Warner died in 1873, leaving the Osburn house to his daughter by will. The Warner home was sold by the executors to Mrs. Harriet Gilmore, wife of Capt. David Gilmore. Here Capt. Gilmore, with his wife and sisters-in-law, Miss Little and Mrs. Mudie, lived for many years. Next door, in the house now owned by Don Rose, Esq., lived another retired river-man, Capt. George W. Cochran, one time burgess and the especial patron of our volunteer firemen whose organization still loyally bears his name as the Cochran Hose Company. The next neighbor of the Osburns to the east and across Graham Street was Jehu P. Smith whose house was on the site later occupied by Mrs. Heck's residence. Mr. Smith, in 1864, bought the house in an unfinished condition from the executors of John Irwin of Irwin Avenue, Allegheny. These four families with two or three more on either side of the railroad comprised all that there was of Sewickley in that immediate neighborhood.

May, 1925.

A FERRY TALE

CLOSE UNDER THE HILLSIDE RAN A CHARMING COUNTRY ROAD

A FERRY TALE

THE STORY OF THE LASHELL AND STOOPS FERRIES

When the Ohio River bridge was opened to traffic in 1911 it put out of service two ferries, Lashell's and Stoops', the one at the foot of Chestnut, the other at Ferry Street, which had long served a public need; now they are but a memory. The lands of Jacob Lashell and William Stoops adjoined on the south side of the river, the two properties having together a river frontage of approximately 3,000 feet. Close under the precipitous hillside and at some elevation above the shore line ran a charming country road bordering the two estates and forming a part of the highway between Middletown (now Coraopolis) and the Narrows Run valley.

Lashell was the earlier landholder of the two and his was probably the first of the two ferries, for the twenty-five acre tract which he bought, April 8, 1847, from Caleb and Eliza Jeffers, adjoining other lands of his which ran back from the river "by the meanderings of Griffith's (or Guffie's) run," was the same for which Henry Ulery on February 14, 1793, received the patent wherein the tract is called "The Ferry." (Guffie's Run," the well-nigh forgotten name of the little stream that tumbles down the ravine a short distance above Stoops Ferry, where formerly the road took a sharp bend inward, passing over a wooden bridge at the foot of "Buttermilk Falls.") Henry Ulery, it will be recalled, was the first white settler on the land which is now part of Sewickley. He held "The Ferry" till December 13, 1814, when he conveyed to Andrew Boggs, from whom Caleb Jeffers bought it, October 7, 1834, and Jeffers, as was said, sold it to Jacob Lashell. It is of interest to note that Henry Ulery, "yeoman," acknowledged his deed before John Way, Justice of the Peace; John Way, who was the son of Caleb Way and grandfather of John Way, Jr., and who in 1810, built the brick house on Beaver Road, below Sand Hill.

THE WILLIAM STOOPS HOUSE

The chain of title ending with William Stoops, on the other hand, begins with a patent to Andrew Boggs, dated January 1st, 1835. From him the land passed to an Andrew Beggs in July of that year, who held it till the year 1857, and he it was who in 1841 built on the property the substantial stone dwelling house that still stands under the cliff-quarry a short distance from the turn of the road back of Stoops Ferry station. Andrew Beggs was succeeded by his son Andrew who in 1862 sold to Thomas S. Guy, but long after he had parted with the property the stone house continued to be known as "the Beggs house."

It does not appear who first operated a ferry at this point but it seems certain that Thomas or "Seat" Guy as he was called and his father, Jacob, did, though no mention of ferry rights occurs in the deed of Thomas S. and Leonore Guy to William Stoops which is dated May 26th, 1869. Lashell's ferry then would seem to have the longer pedigree; but be that as it may, Stoops ferry undoubtedly was the older and more frequented crossing point, being directly opposite the mouth of the Narrows run ravine by way of which, tradition says, the Indians passed to and fro between the trail which is now the Brodhead Road and the great Fort Pitt, Fort McIntosh, Sandusky, Detroit trail which skirted the river on its northern shore. The Narrows run ravine was a natural gateway to the Indian country lying north and east of the Ohio river, and the canoe here furnished the connecting link between two great and well marked trails.

It was in the year 1865 that William Stoops and his wife, Nancy, moved to Sewickley from the home of their pioneer ancestors on the banks of Chartiers Creek. The story of Jenny Stoops, great-grandmother of William, as told in Charles McKnight's *Our Western Border* and as handed down by tradition in the family today, is a thrilling one. Jennie and her husband, James Stoops, lived in a cabin some five miles distant from Fort Pitt. It was in the summer of 1780, during the husband's absence at the fort, that the Indians in a night attack burned the cabin and made off with Jennie and her baby boy.

James on his return followed their trail down the river, crossing, it is believed, at the very place where, years later, Stoops Ferry was to be located. The Indians were evidently following the Fort McIntosh trail, and Stoops pressed forward with his companions hoping to overtake the band. It happened that Captain Sam Brady, General Brodhead's trusted scout and friend of the settlers, was returning from an expedition to the north. Approaching Fort McIntosh from the north he was following the trail when suddenly he was aware of a number of Indians advancing on horseback. He hid and as they drew near he saw that one of the savages was carrying a baby while another had mounted behind him, a white woman.

Catching the woman's eye Brady motioned to her to hold her head back and, aiming at the Indian, he fired and killed him, seized the woman and made his escape. Being himself disguised as an Indian, the woman said to him, "Why did you kill your brother?" He replied, "Jennie Stoops, don't you know me, Captain Sam Brady?" Jennie and her husband were soon re-united but nothing was heard of the child for three years. One evening an old Indian came to their cabin and asked them to trade him a gun and a white horse, offering to tell them where the boy was. A bargain was struck and the lad was brought back, but he had become so used to Indian ways that it was long before he could be made to feel at home or be persuaded to sleep indoors. The child grew to manhood and was the grandfather of William Stoops of Stoops Ferry.

Mr. Stoops on coming to Sewickley bought from Capt. John C. Anderson a sixty foot lot on Beaver Street, east of Division Street with the brick dwelling which had been Capt. Anderson's home for eight years. We of today remember it as Dr. Chantler's house, formerly occupying the site of the present residence of Mr. George R. McDonald, No. 537 Beaver Street. Here Mr. Stoops had as his next door neighbor Mr. John Miller who well remembers him today. Down by the river at the foot of Ferry Street was a sawmill owned and operated by Joe Banks, Samuel McMaster and Henry Warner which they had bought from "Seat" Guy and his father "Jake." This sawmill William Stoops bought, and soon thereafter he purchased from Guy the ferry rights and the land across the river with the stone dwelling house, where he made his home, and where he died on August 20th, 1879.

Jacob Lashell and William Stoops did not actually operate their ferries. Each employed a ferryman to handle the skiffs and flats. Mr. Jolly who for so many years ran Lashell's ferry will be remembered by many who can picture him as he rowed leisurely across the river, sitting sideways on the thwart for the purpose of more easy expectoration down stream. Do any recall Syd Sawyer, Mr. Stoop's ferryman, a silent philosopher who knew every skiff, barge, towboat and packet on the river?

Close to the stone dwelling house there was a country store the site of which is now covered by the tracks of the Lake Erie railroad; a little country store where folks came to trade and gossip; farmers down from Sharon (now Carnot), with butter, eggs and berries. It was on a bench in front of this store that Syd Sawyer, the ferryman, sat all day long silently chewing his natural leaf Virginia tobacco and whittling a stick. Here he had a full view of all the river craft and could respond to a hail from either shore summoning him to his intermittent duties as ferryman.

Entrusting the ferry to Sawyer, Mr. Stoops devoted himself to the busy life of a river captain. He owned and ran at different times several steamboats; the last one, which he had built at Pringle's boatyard up the Monongahela, he named the *J. S. Pringle,* after its builder. It was of unusual design, having two engines and two stern wheels, one of which could be stopped or reversed while the other went ahead thus enabling the boat to "turn on a ten cent piece." The only other boat on the river of similar design had been built by Samuel Young, father of Mr. Ezra Young of Edgeworth.

The *J. S. Pringle* ran in the Pittsburgh-St. Louis trade carrying passengers and 700 to 800 tons of freight. Captain Stoops ran also to New Orleans, and was active in his river interests down to the time of his death in 1879. In only one

WILLIAM STOOPS
(Photograph by Sperber)

venture did he fail of success. He made the experiment of a steam ferry, but the amount of business did not justify the expense, and moreover the operator was required to carry a pilot's license, which was a bit beyond Syd Sawyer's attainments.

Five years after Captain Stoops's death his widow parted with the title to the property and the old stone house came into the possession of one Jeremiah Meek, who took by the same conveyance "all the rights, liberties, privileges and franchises connected with or necessary to the proper enjoyment of the ferry—etc." The naming of the station "Stoops

JACOB LASHELL
(Photograph by Dabbs)

Ferry" by the Pittsburgh & Lake Erie Railroad has preserved the historic traditions which were also recognized in the chartering of the Stoops Ferry Bridge Company in 1903 by Joseph W. Craig, Charles W. Baker and Percy L. Craig. This project, capitalized at $100,000.00, came to naught as did two other incorporations by the same gentlemen in that year, the Crescent Bridge Company and the Osborne Bridge Company, proposing to cross the river at Leetsdale and at Glen Osborne.

Jacob Lashell looked to the river for a livelihood as did William Stoops, though in a different fashion. He had the income from his ferry and his earnings as mate on one or another of the river steamboats, but more important than these sources of gain were his ventures down the river, as far as New Orleans, carrying potatoes and other farm produce which he bought on Neville Island and floated down in flat boats which he had built for the purpose. Arrived at the end of his journey he would sell the flat for its lumber and come north to repeat the operation another year.

He was an enterprising man; his versatility was shown when he gathered together a string of horses and drove them over the mountains to Philadelphia for sale. He died April 11, 1886, since when most of his land has passed into other hands, though descendants still retain some. In 1892 his sons John and George with two other incorporators secured a charter for the Lashell Ferry Company "located more than 3000 feet from any other ferry." Then in 1911 the highway bridge was built, and the Lashell and Stoops ferries both passed into the limbo of half-forgotten things.

September, 1928.

HARBAUGH'S POND

HARBAUGH'S POND

AN OLD SEWICKLEY PLAY CENTER

THEY are filling in Harbaugh's pond. You don't hear this shouted from the house-tops nor yet discussed in whispers. In fact, nobody notices it or cares. "Harbaugh's Pond" means nothing at all to the present generation. Only the firm that has the contract for excavating the site of the new hospital is in the least interested, its truck-loads of earth and shale finding there a convenient place of disposal. Behind the freight station and extending eastwardly from Chestnut Street the fill is gradually approaching street level and soon another old favorite playground will have completely disappeared.

"Harbaugh's Pond"—that little depression by the roadside? Yes, but once it was more than that. Formerly there were only two railroad tracks and the ground fell away immediately back of the station which was located about where the present freight station now stands, so that the lowland had quite a respectable width and, extending in length from Chestnut Street almost to Pine and sometimes quite that far, it held a considerable body of water. In summer the pond was the home of hosts of tuneful frogs and the breeding place of swarms of mosquitoes. (Every bedroom in those days had a hook in the ceiling above the bed from which hung a mosquito bar that swept to the floor.) The bottom of the pond was of blue clay, too sticky and tenacious for pleasant wading and apt to seize and hold the pole of any daring youngster who pushed his raft out on a voyage to the muskrat island off-shore.

In winter time the pond was at its best, for then it was gay with skaters: boys and girls and an occasional grown-up, all on strapped skates. Today, above the rising tide of earth, still stands on the south bank the old locust tree where we used to put on our skates, screwing them round and round till they were fast to the heel, if we hadn't already strapped them to our copper-toed shoes before leaving the warmth of the home kitchen, clumping down to the pond over the frozen ground. Some were the envied possessors of "club" skates which fitted into an iron plate let into the heel and were clamped to the sole with a key. There were not lacking graceful and expert skaters. One of the best remembered was Joseph Warren, the telegrapher and station agent, whose intricate ice patterns were the admiration of all. Lively hockey games were staged there by the older boys, though none had heard it called hockey; it was "shinny," and the best shinny sticks were to be found on the slope of Cemetery Hill or up at "Miller and Dickson's." (What has become of that word "haley" by the way, meaning the goal?) No, the winters weren't any colder than those of today, for there is recollection of recurring thaws when the ice bent underfoot and you skated as on a carpet, uphill at every stroke, with the water gradually seeping through till you made waves like a boat. Then suddenly the strain would become too great and the last venturesome lad would break through and get a thorough ducking, to the unbounded delight of the rest of the gang.

The pond was gradually decreasing in size; it had seen its best days. Even the old muskrat had gone whose winter home in the midst of the waters made an island, convenient for the skaters' bonfire. Then it was that we listened to the tales of long ago when the pond was in its heyday of skating carnivals at night, of fancy costumes, brilliant lights, bonfires on shore 'n' everything. For Harbaugh's pond in the very early 'Seventies—and before—had attained the dignity of a cared-for and supervised skating rink. Under a special dispensation from Mr. Harbaugh, a group of the boys undertook to keep the ice clear of snow and to police the place generally. They built a set of steps down from Chestnut Street and put up a small rest-house with coal stove and skate lockers, all the privileges of which, together with that of the ice, were secured by the purchase of a season ticket. This efficient management continued through several seasons, and the picture of those gay times is bright in the memory of some today. Ask about it and see the twinkle of merriment as recollection brings back the ballooning of hoop-skirts and the flashing of peg-top trousers as the girls and boys of those days frolicked on the pond.

In later times the steps and rest-house were no more, and the main approach to the pond was from Chestnut Street at the railroad crossing, down a slight grade from the tracks by a road that led to a freight siding. John Howard's little store stood at the corner about on the spot now occupied by the gateman's tower. "Pop" Howard was a colored man, short and well-rounded, with grayish hair; a kind-hearted friend of the boys and girls, all of whom were fond of him. His sign read: "Candy. Pies. Hair Cut," and, desiring one or another of these commodities, you stepped down abruptly into the shop where you were offered a tempting selection of stick candy of the barber pole variety, "lickerish" root and peppermint "lozengers" from the glass jars on the counter, a cent's worth the usual purchase. Or he would at your request dig out from within the show-case pink strips of cocoanut candy or other of the more perishable stock. Sometimes these after Pop's handling carried a faint suggestion of bay rum, for his barber shop, a little room possibly ten by twelve, was right next to the candy store, a doorway between. Unpretentious it was and primitive in its appointments, the one barber shop of the town. Today you will find men of rising years and dignified matrons who recall with a smile the visits they regularly made in their childhood to Pop Howard's hair cutting establishment. Here as you sat in the operating chair you looked out through the window upon the waters of the pond. Fifteen cents was the price of a hair cut; not exorbitant, considering that Pop had a monopoly. Simplicity marked the interior furnishings, a few chromos on the walls and a busy woodchopper toy fastened to the stovepipe and operated by the heat which rose from the stove. Pop furnished no reading matter to his patrons. The Police Gazette as an innovation came later, introduced by a rival shop—where hair cuts were raised to twenty cents.

The last skating on Harbaugh's pond was in 1882, or 1883, for the pond was drained about then by means of a connection made with the sewer on Chestnut Street. Ask George ("Jersey") Little if he remembers it. He should. You'll find him, one of Sewickley's three surviving Civil War veterans, faithfully holding down his job as night watchman on the Ohio river bridge. "Jersey" and Tom Cunningham were at work in the trench that was cut many feet deep in the sandy loam when suddenly the sides caved in and buried them. Feverishly the other men dug down to rescue them. Cunningham was dead when found and small hope remained for Jersey when, most surprisingly, he appeared at the end of the trench whither he had crawled through the sewer pipe. I wonder if he thinks of that experience as he sees the old pond being filled and leveled up.

Harbaugh's pond is gone. It was only a memory anyhow, and that memory we may still cherish even though its very site has now disappeared under the march of progress. It is better so.

March 1928.

ON THE WAY TO SCHOOL

Where Mrs. Mudie had her school. This picture was taken later, in Dr. Benton's time.

ON THE WAY TO SCHOOL

WHAT A LOITERING BOY SAW

One of Sewickley's private schools of the late 'Seventies was that conducted by Mrs. E. L. Mudie in the Episcopal Sunday School building on the site of the St. Stephen's Parish House. It was a one-story frame structure, its floor-plan in the form of a cross with the entrance on Vine Street, now Frederick Avenue, about opposite Dr. Mitchell's present office. To the west of the school stood the frame church near the Christy line, while on the Broad Street side was an open lot shut in by a high paling fence and with boardwalks around it. Here was ample room for such games as "black-man," "prisoners' base" and even for a pint-size ball game where "over the fence was out." Happy were the youngsters who here received their first initiation into the mysteries of the three R's at the hands of a kind and gentle teacher.

From all parts of the village the children came. Let us in imagination accompany the contingent from below the railroad and note the landmarks as we pass. There was, first, Harbaugh's pond, bordering Chestnut Street, with its seductive allure of muskrat and tadpoles. At the crossing of the two railroad tracks stood John Howard's candy store and barber shop, where you stepped down below the street level to inspect his stock of candies, and as chewing gum had not yet come into vogue, a cent's worth of stick candy was the usual purchase. If time allowed, a side excursion might be indulged in to explore the dim interior of the pump-house, a high brick building to the east of the station where two wells, popularly believed to be one hundred feet deep, fascinated one with their hollow reverberations. These wells supplied water for the engines which pulled up and stopped at the tanks. Tramps frequented this spot, waiting for a lift to points east or west, and here you might read their records carved on platform and on tank timbers, such pseudonyms as "Kansas Shorty," "Omaha Bill" and other dime novel penknife names. Here, too, the long cattle trains coming in from the west would on hot summer days puff slowly by so that the suffering animals might be showered with a gush of cold water. The passenger station was then located about where the present freight station stands, to the east of Chestnut Street. It was of red brick with a wide wooden platform extending out to the rails where stood a tall square post carrying a red banner-signal at its top. Benches for passengers ranged along the wall beneath the porch, while inside were two waiting rooms, one for men and one for women and children, with a semi-circular ticket office between them where Joseph Warren, station agent and telegrapher, presided for so many years. Across the tracks was the freight and baggage platform, four or five steps above street level, with a small baggage room at the western end close to the Chestnut Street sidewalk.

Leaving the attractions of the railroad and paying heed to the sign that warns us to "Look out for the Locomotive," we cross the tracks, turn west on Bank Street and pass, on the left, the old one-story frame building that had formerly been the station, which now stood about half way between Chestnut Street and the site of the present one. This building served as council chamber and jail, the city fathers occupying one room and the guests of the municipality the other. You pause to listen and even venture to peep in at the window if perchance you might catch a glimpse of some forlorn derelict locked in there to sober up. About where the station now stands there was a small frame house past which ran the drive that led across the tracks into the Colonel McKelvy place, now the Park Place Hotel. The remains of that driveway are still to be seen, extending from the station platform to the trolley stop.

Now we turn up Broad Street passing Judge White's apple orchard which reached from Bank Street to a point nearly opposite Vine Street with an entrance driveway directly across from the present Dorian Club. This led to the White homestead, a portion of which still stands on Melville Lane surrounded by modern dwellings. On the Bank Street corner opposite was the home of "Old Man Reed" who earned the enmity of all youngsters each winter season by spreading ashes on his sidewalk where we coasted past his entrance gate. Later we had our revenge, when the old man, then away past seventy, set forth on a strangely romantic treasure hunt somewhere along the Atlantic coast, where his body was later found. The building now the Dorian Club was then the residence of D. N. ("Deacon") White, editor of the Pittsburgh *Daily Gazette* and widely known as the "Father of the Republican Party." (He it was who issued the call for the first convention of the party which met in 1856 in old Lafayette Hall at the corner of Wood Street and Fourth Avenue, Pittsburgh.) Next to Deacon White's house was an open lot and then on the corner of Vine Street (now Frederick) behind the usual paling fence and gate posts stood the residence of F. M. Hutchinson, later to be crowned by him with a mansard roof. That vacant lot where now stands the St. James Parochial School was shut off from view by a fence of wide boards set upright which could however be scaled in case of necessity, as when Mr. Hutchinson, captain of some military organization from the city, drilled his company there, his two sons, also in uniform and gold lace, marching at his side to the anguished envy of the spectators on the fence top.

We are almost at the school now and have come to the Graham house (Mr. Gilchrist's residence today), a clapboarded dwelling with a low picket fence in front. The gate opens and little old Prof. Anderson steps out on his way to the Academy where he is a teacher. We fear that he will be late as he has a long walk ahead of him and it is almost time for school to "take in." Here come the youngsters from other parts of the village hurrying down Broad Street. They have passed old "Chapultepec" Sample's home (now the Wessenauer Flower Shop) where lived our sole surviving veteran of the Mexican War, with his wooden leg "mowing the grass" as we irreverently dubbed his sidewheel gait. Farther on their way were the homes of Dr. Johnston and Dr. Burns and the house on the corner of Thorn Street with its woodshed close to the sidewalk. Across from it stood the old Methodist church, later to be torn down to make way for the present building; then came the parsonage close by, and, a little further along, the United Presbyterian church with its twin spires or towers. Now come Lent and Easter, side by side, for John Lent, the florist, lived in the house now the residence of our burgess, O. S. Richardson, Esq., and next door to Lent, the Reverend Easter, rector of St. Stephen's.

But we must not keep Mrs. Mudie waiting, although our tardiness would receive the mildest of reproofs. There she stands in the doorway, bell in hand; she rings, and we cross the dusty street, filing into the school-room to take up another day's march along the Highway of Learning.

May, 1928.

THE FRIENDLY RIVER

THE FRIENDLY RIVER

THE FRIENDLY RIVER

RECOLLECTIONS OF BOY LIFE IN AND ON THE OHIO

SEWICKLEY no longer possesses a water-front; the old Ohio river beach is gone. The shelving expanse of pebbles that extended from Glen Osborne to Chestnut Street, with the willow-covered river frontage farther down-stream, has completely disappeared under a deep cover of earth and cinders deposited there by the steam shovels that are preparing the railroad's new right-of-way. Another natural feature is thus sacrificed in the inexorable march of progress. Time was when the river and its beach were the delight of all Sewickley boys both great and small; one might say the chief delight, for strange as it may seem to the present generation, the river and its interests once occupied a foremost place in the affections of the youth of the Valley. At all seasons of the year it furnished recreation of one kind or another, swimming and rowing in the summer and skating in winter, while in spring and fall the beach with its piles of driftwood invited to the enjoyment of roaring fires where potatoes were to be baked and an occasional jack salmon broiled and eaten with a gusto that the absence of salt failed to diminish. The first swim of the season some time in May, and the last usually in late September though too cold for real enjoyment, were the occasion of much pardonable boasting, while in the regular summer season no day went by, Sundays included, without its troop of youngsters splashing and shouting in the river, running up and down the beach, or diving from barge or towboat that chanced to be tied up awaiting the return of high water. To run barefoot on those beach pebbles called for soles like shoe leather, but these were soon acquired since all boys in those days said farewell to shoes in early spring. Bathing suits were, of course, unheard of, excepting when parties of sedate older folk resorted to the river on summer evenings—and such improvised bathing suits as did then appear! Just to play about on the beach was a delight; collecting strange kinds of pebbles, lucky stones with holes through them, fossils that we called "coral" and that red or orange-colored "keel" so convenient for writing and marking on board fences and on house walls. Then there were crawfish to catch, springs of cold water to dig for and "trot-lines" to set, pulling them in next day with now and then a jack salmon on one end of their many hooks. But, after all, the swim was the thing. Mr. Bruce Tracy's barges below Chestnut Street were the favorite resort for those who enjoyed diving, but for the real experts in that line the upper deck of a steamboat or the topmost bucket of its stern wheel was none too high. Then there was old Stevenson's scow to swim from if he weren't around; the old flat that he pushed before him, wading waist deep and picking up the round stones that he sold in Pittsburgh as paving or cobble stones. Stevenson was crabbed by reputation, a hater of youth, one who would steal your clothes, it was said, besides giving you a round of profanity if he caught you near his flatboat. Occasionally a great lumber raft would appear from the far upper reaches of the Allegheny, a beautiful sight, like a floating island quietly drifting with the current, the two big sweeps at the bow and stern guiding it around the bends, and in the middle a board wigwam, the living quarters of the half dozen rough lumbermen that composed its crew. Great sport and exciting it was to swim out and clamber aboard, to run up and down on the clean pine boards and dive off before you were carried too far downstream.

It was no great feat to swim the river in time of low water, and when the river was particularly shallow it could be waded afoot or on horseback at the riffle opposite Osborn station. Rowing vied with swimming as the favorite summer sport, the field of adventure extending from the Riffle to Dead Man's Island. Both of these landmarks (or water marks?) have now been done away with. The current at the riffle was too swift to stem with oars, though by clinging to the timbers of the wing dam that extended down stream near the far shore of the river you could work your skiff up to quiet water and so to the "back river" above Middletown now called Coraopolis. Then, returning, you enjoyed a short dash down through the swift water and a quiet row to the home port. The only excitement comparable to this was to row out and into the second or third wave behind the stern wheel of a steamboat.

In winter time the skating was not associated especially with the freezing over of the river, though that sometimes occurred, but was enjoyed here and there in more or less sheltered coves like that just below "Tracy's abutment" at the foot of Chestnut Street, although occasionally continuous stretches of available ice along shore lured the youngsters as far as Little Sewickley Creek and beyond. Especially fortunate was it when one could cross the river and enjoy the larger field of ice that lay within the wing dam. Usually however this was inaccessible as Lashell's ferry opposite Chestnut Street would be out of service at such times because of floating ice. Lashell's ferry, where you shouted "Over" and old Mr. Jolly, the ferryman, would row across for you, charging fifteen cents the round trip.

Interest in the river was not confined to these summer and winter sports. There was the river traffic with its towboats and packets, the former guiding great fleets of coal barges, and the passenger packets with deck, "texas" and pilot house trimmed with fancy woodwork and gleaming in white paint. Every boy kept a list of the boats he had seen. Their names and appearance were familiar to all, and many a lad could distinguish them by their whistle, or even by their manner of puffing, before they came within sight around the bend. The *Boaz* with its fancy pilot house, the *R. J. Grace, Nellie Walton, Tom Dodsworth, Katie Stockdale, Buckeye State*—any boy could run through a score of these from memory. Once in a great while a boat would come up from the lower river, beyond Cincinnati, or even from the Mississippi, and then great was the excitement and bitter the disappointment of those who missed the sight. On the rare occasions when a packet made a landing at Chestnut Street it was an opportunity to dash up the gangplank among the real southern darky roustabouts, to be chased off with a rush when the starting bell sounded or when the mud clerk lost his temper. Then there was the little steamer that was always warmly welcomed on its somewhat rare visits, the "Lighthouse Tender Lily." Like "Light Horse Harry Lee" the name itself sounded sweetly on the tongue. Shyly we recognized something poetic in her name, "Tender Lily," the word "Lighthouse" not registering particularly, and it was not till after years that we realized that the government boat *Lily* was merely a lighthouse tender bringing lamp oil and supplies up river to the numerous shore lights.

In early spring the first of the jo-boats appeared, usually with a tin type "gallery" attached. Here you disposed of your winter's accumulation of old iron, glass bottles, etc., in return for which you had your picture taken—no extra charge for the dog— or you accepted a bit of pressed glassware, say a pair of salt cellars in the shape of swans or elephants or something equally graceful and artistic. The jo-boat man fixed the price of your scrap iron and you took whatever he bid for it. Then there were the boat clubs whose members were the proud possessors of paper racing shells in which they skimmed the surface of the waters on summer evenings, in training for imaginary race meets. A real boat race now and then furnished a thrill, as when John Lynch, the village champion, met some rival oarsman from one of the Pittsburgh clubs; and when Captain Paul Boynton gaily paddled by on his way to New Orleans in his inflated rubber bathing suit and towing his diminutive supply boat christened *Baby Mine*, the beach was lined with cheering spectators.

Why, the river teemed with varied interests the year round! Its sleepy low water in summer time and its wild freshets in winter and spring, all of its moods met a response in our daily lives. It was the central fact in our boyhood existence. Whether roaming the beaches under the hot summer sun, playing Indian on the mud flats back of the dam, or in winter-time standing on the shore ice with "hawking pole" struggling to bring ashore saw-log or lumber as it floated by, the River was our great playground; and today—how many give it a thought; how many have even noticed that Sewickley has lost her waterfront?

March, 1928.

THE BELVA DEARS

WINCHESTER DANA OSGOOD

THE BELVA DEARS

AN INCIDENT OF THE BELVA LOCKWOOD CAMPAIGN

BRIGADIER General Frederick Funston in his *Memories of Two Wars* writes of the fall of Guiamaro, an episode of the Cuban War of 1896, and incidentally tells of the death of Major Winchester Dana Osgood, commanding the Cuban artillery, who was killed while in the act of sighting a 12-pounder in the thick of the fight. Win Osgood was a Sewickley boy back in the 'Eighties and ten years later was known throughout the college world as a brilliant foot-ball star at Cornell and at the University of Pennsylvania. His name brings up recollections of a campaign and a fracas here in Sewickley in which he took a prominent part.

* * * *

It was in the fall of 1884, during the Blaine-Cleveland presidential campaign, that Mrs. Belva Lockwood, a prominent lawyer of Washington, D. C., and a strong advocate of what was known in that day as "women's rights," forced her way into the lime-light by announcing her candidacy for the office of President of the United States. The cry of "women's rights" was not taken very seriously then by the general public and Mrs. Lockwood's campaign came in for a great deal of more or less flippant comment.

Taking their cue from their elders, it occurred to some of the Sewickley youngsters to organize a mock Belva Lockwood Club in honor of the first woman to be nominated for the presidency. Torch-light parades were a feature of political campaigns then and a marching club was the natural outcome of a meeting held one evening at "Reed's corner," Broad and Bank streets, where a membership of some twenty-five or thirty boys was enrolled. Dave Murdoch was elected captain, Harry ("Happy") Gilson, Ed. McMillen and George Sommerville, lieutenants, and shortly thereafter drilling began on the river bank back of the Nevin home. Every day after school hours the work went on, until the company had pretty well mastered the problem of alignment and this was about all the tactics that were aspired to, besides keeping step. Chief interest was centered in the uniform, or more properly, the costume, the twenty-five or thirty varying ideas and opinions finally simmering down to agreement upon white Mother Hubbard gowns with red yokes, the ensemble topped with blue sun bonnets of the poke variety, while each "Belva Dear" was to carry a new broom equipped with a kerosene torch. The profoundest secrecy was maintained, only "Billy" Chivers, the tailor, being taken into their confidence and given the contract for some two score uniforms. Greatly did the old man enjoy his part in the undertaking and scarcely could he ply his needle and thread for chuckling as the boys dropped in for their fittings.

The date of the parade was fixed for the night of October 30th; citizens along the line of march were tipped off and promised to burn red fire in honor of the occasion. Then came a surprise. Somehow the Pittsburgh *Leader* got wind of the proceedings, and, as it happened that Mrs. Belva Lockwood herself was due to pass through Pittsburgh that day the *Leader* people sent word to her that a woman's suffrage demonstration was to be held in Sewickley, preceded by a parade of a club named in her honor. Could she stop over and attend the ceremonies? She replied that her engagements would not permit, but that in passing through Sewickley she would throw from her train a message of greeting to the Belva Lockwood Club. This she did; the eager committee at the railroad crossing captured the bit of paper and, it must be confessed, felt just a twinge of remorse when they noted the earnestness of the message. Mrs. Lockwood, not suspecting the burlesque nature of the plans, wrote as follows:

"On the train from Pittsburgh, October 29, '84.

"Chairman, Ladies and Gentlemen of Belva Lockwood Club:

"I send cheers and congratulations for your demonstration tonight. It means equal rights for men and women, equal political privileges, and equal civil rights under the law. It means harmony between capital and labor, and a reform in the money system of the country. Reading has an Equal Rights mass meeting tonight for the same purpose, and Cumberland tomorrow night. I address the people of Flint, Mich., tomorrow evening.

"Yours truly,
"BELVA A. LOCKWOOD."

The parade came off as scheduled, though the muddy condition of the then unpaved streets necessitated the addition of rubber boots to the regulation uniform. Headed by drum and fife, the march began in Maple Lane and extended over the principal streets of the village. The lighted transparency carried well to the front was a work of art. The inscriptions on its four sides were: "Lockwood and Howe Club, of Sewickley." "Women's Equal Rights." "The Fair Belva Dears" and "Give Us a Vote!" Along the entire line of march the procession was greeted with red fire and great enthusiasm, the latter gradually resolving itself into jeers and cat-calls as the attending mob grew larger and the point of disbanding drew near. At last, as the unattached grew bolder, apples and overripe vegetables began to get the range. The transparency was too good a mark, and it was soon riddled, while its guardian, proudly bearing it aloft, received a turnip full on the yoke of his Mother Hubbard, and "Happy" Gilson was bleeding from a cut on the head. When the railroad crossing at Pine Street was finally reached all semblance of an orderly march was abandoned and a free-for-all pitched battle began. Here was where Win Osgood came out strong. He was probably the smallest Belva of them all, but stockily built and full of fight. Thrusting his broom into the hands of a bystander, and shouting, "Here, hold my torch," he plunged into the thickest of the fight in a whirl of muddy skirts and rubber boots. He went after the leader of the mob, a chap twice his size, with such suddenness of onslaught as to turn the tide of battle and enable the marchers to gather their scattering forces and reach the drill ground in more or less dignified retreat, where they disbanded. Thus passed into history the Lockwood and Howe Marching Club, of Sewickley; "The second Lockwood Club in the United States," as the *Leader* boasted the next day, a similar organization having been formed in some New Jersey town.

Lieutenant (later Brigadier General) Osgood, Win's father, soon after removed from Sewickley with his family, Win entering Cornell and later the University of Pennsylvania where, whatever his scholastic attainments may have been, his athletic prowess was acclaimed throughout the world of sport. Old graduates of "Penn," and of their athletic rivals, will recall how the cheering sections rang with the pulsating yell, "Who's good? Os-good! The whole—damn—team's good!" The fall of 1895 saw him the gridiron hero of the University and one year later he gave his life to the cause of Cuban liberty. Always impulsive, always eager for the fray, whether in peace or in war-time, Winchester Dana Osgood first showed his mettle in the memorable battle of the Belva Dears of 1884.

November, 1910.

McDONALD'S GROVE

McDONALD'S GROVE

BUSH MEETINGS; TEMPERANCE RALLIES; SUMMER NIGHT CONCERTS
AND DANCING IN THE 'EIGHTIES

Down on Maple Lane between the railroad and the river bank stands the frame dwelling that was formerly the home of Captain J. Sharp McDonald, a retired rivermen and in his day one of the best known citizens of Sewickley, whose widow, a gifted singer, is still with us, honored and respected by the entire community. Originally the McDonald home stood alone in the center of a tract of about seven acres, which extended from the railroad down to low water mark on the Ohio river. Lawn, shade trees and meadow beautified the front, towards the railroad, while between the rear of the dwelling and the steep river bank there grew a number of stately oaks with chestnut and hickory trees forming what was known as "McDonald's grove."

CAPT. J. SHARP McDONALD

Quite a considerable grove it was, entirely clear of underbrush with a soft carpet of grass between the massive tree trunks and here and there a patch of bluets and a bit of moss to give it a forest look. The grove was by no means a public park, yet the genial proprietor made no objection to its enjoyment by all, not excepting the youngsters of the neighborhood. Gatherings of various sorts were held here. Sometimes a platform and speakers' stand were built for services religious or semi-religious in character. The grass extended to the edge of the cliff overlooking the river where a set of steep steps led down to the gravelly beach. An ideal spot it was, especially at night when one left the circle of candle lanterns surrounding the platform and strolled out into the moonlight to enjoy the view of the quietly flowing river below.

Occasionally of a summer Sunday afternoon the colored folk of the valley would hold religious services here; "bush meetings" they were called, where the unrestrained singing and praying and the shouted "Amens" awakened echoes from the hills across the river. Then again as the backwash of the "Francis Murphy Movement" disturbed the tranquillity of our village pool, great temperance meetings were held in the grove, when the best known and most sincere drinkers of the community would rise and give their "experience," perhaps weep a bit, then sign the pledge to an accompaniment of hymns and approving shouts, while we of the younger element, caught up in the general excitement, would in our turn file up to the speakers' stand to add the weight of our approval to the verdict against the demon rum, signing the pledge "never to use whisky as a beverage." We may not have had a very clear notion as to the exact meaning of the word "beverage" but—the applause was thrilling and the pledge card with its fancy Old English lettering and gilt trimmings was quite attractive, and besides—everybody was doing it. So, we signed up for the rest of our lives. Like the bush meetings these gatherings were held on Sunday afternoons and they served quite effectively to liven up those otherwise rather oppressive periods of somnolence, those summer Sunday afternoons whose hush was almost audible, and only accentuated by the mournful note of a dove or the distant crowing of some lonely rooster. The "church train" had returned from the city and all was quiet along the railroad, when there would come a burst of singing from the grove with an accompaniment of piano or violin, the opening shout of the exhorter, and the spell was broken; the world woke up again and was glad. With all due respect for the good old days it must be admitted that the old-fashioned Sabbath afternoons just verged on the dull.

The decade before the Gay Nineties was not lacking in diversions. McDonald's grove was the scene of brilliant social affairs, of musical evenings when John and Charlie Gernert brought their orchestra from the city and gave seasons of summer night concerts there. A large platform was built, a piano and folding chairs installed and the weather man importuned. Following the musical program the platform was cleared for dancing which was kept up till the last train summoned the orchestra back to town. The waltz and polka shared the stage with square dances, the quadrille and lancers. It was not considered too old-fashioned to have the figures called for the latter by a member of the committee in charge who stood on a chair beside the leader of the orchestra. The favorite "figure caller" is today one of our prominent citizens, our burgess, in fact, who can testify to the truth of the assertion that the Elegant Eighties were socially all that could be desired. The grove on these festal occasions was a scene of beauty with Chinese lanterns lighting up the dancing floor and dimly revealing the dark tree trunks in the background, the contrast of evening gowns and formal dress with the out-of-door surroundings making a picture long to be remembered. These seasons of summer night concerts continued for a number of years and were distinctly the high spots of Sewickley's social life. We wonder if Rear Admiral Charles B. McVay of the United States Navy, a former Sewickley boy, ever harks back in memory to a certain summer of dances in McDonald's grove when he and a party of his fellow middies from Annapolis with their uniforms and gold braid put the civilian beaux completely out of the running and turned the heads of all of the girls! Dull? No, the 'Eighties were not dull.

"REDDING UP"

The summer over, the youngsters under dancing age came into their own, for then arrived the nutting season and it never occurred to them that the nuts were not their property. In the fall, after a night of frost, the early morning would find numerous small boys busily gathering their harvest of shellbarks and chestnuts. It is pleasant to record that Mr. McDonald, the owner of the grove, told some of us in after years that he enjoyed our sport as much as we did, often watching us from his window, and that once when his "hired man" (so called in those days) had gathered the nuts before we arrived he made him scatter them on the ground again so that we youngsters might not meet disappointment in our search.

* * * *

What a delightful part in the life of the community McDonald's grove played; childhood, youth and age resorting to it in pursuit of their varied interests; the scene of nutting parties, of social affairs and of fervent religious gatherings. The remnants of two or three of those old trees still stand, vainly endeavoring to furnish shade and shelter to the dwellings that have sprung up there, but the grove itself is gone and with it has departed much of the simplicity that once marked the social life of Sewickley.

April, 1928.

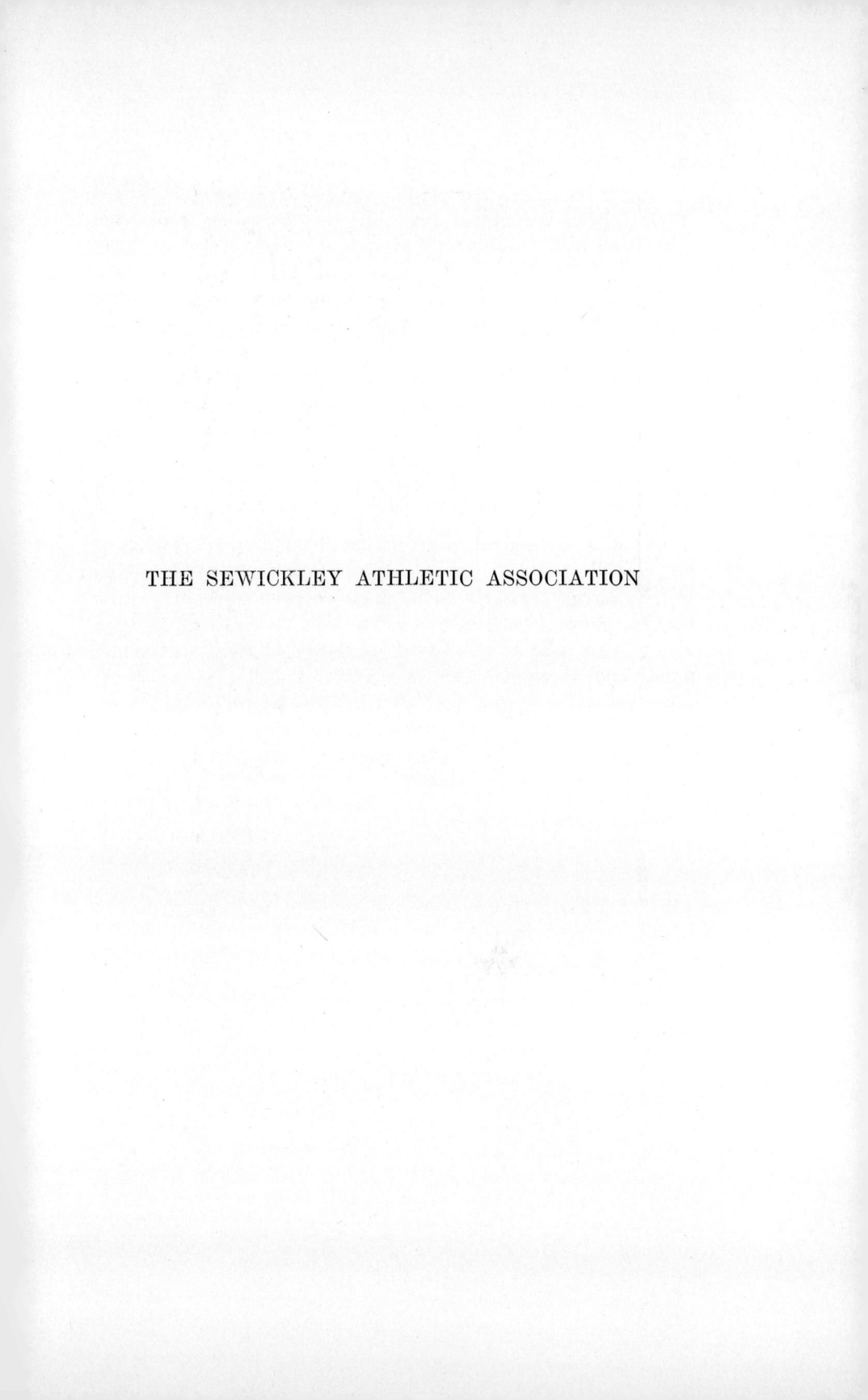

THE SEWICKLEY ATHLETIC ASSOCIATION

THE ATHLETIC GROUNDS
Reproduced from *The Qui Vive*, 1885

THE SEWICKLEY ATHLETIC ASSOCIATION

THE RECREATIONAL AND SOCIAL CENTER IN THE 'EIGHTIES AND 'NINETIES

BASEBALL was the one great sport indulged in by the youth of Sewickley in the 'Seventies. The game had become popular in the colleges and when the summer vacations brought home the fortunate few "college men" they gave a great impetus to the athletic movement, particularly on the ball field. Not that there were lacking ball nines of stay-at-home talent some of which, notably the La Belles, the Crescents and others, carried their fame afar; others not so widely celebrated named themselves for some popular local merchant whose patronage was evidenced by the gift of uniforms and equipment. The F. A. Myers and the C. P. Miles ball clubs were of that category, honoring Mr. Myers, the hardware dealer, whose store occupied the present site of the Peoples Bank and "Charley Miles," the proprietor of the drug store on the opposite corner. The college boys, however, infused new life in the game and introduced its latest developments. Great was the sensation when a young college pitcher displayed an uncanny ability to strike out the batsmen with what surely appeared to be a curve ball. The fairness of this was questioned and he was ruled out of the pitcher's box in some games and relegated to the outfield. Various vacant lots were resorted to for match games, the most popular and the largest one being the Sands and Adair field on the south side of Frederick Avenue between Walnut and Little Streets, the backstop near Walnut and the outfield in the slight depression at Little. Here was played many a hard fought match. Gloves, masks and chest protectors were unknown, yet the catcher caught "off the bat" and hot liners were fielded with bare hands. Old timers will recall one of the crack catchers on the Sands and Adair lot, afterwards a well-known preacher, whose bloody fingers were tied up in rags as the game progressed but who continued to catch through the full nine innings.

Gradually this playing ground was encroached upon by buildings and the game languished for a time. Then, in the spring of 1882, a well attended meeting was held at the residence of Mr. Cass Carpenter "for the purpose of organizing an athletic club for the cultivation of outdoor amusements." A constitution was drafted, the name "Sewickley Athletic Association" adopted and officers chosen for the first year: Mr. Carpenter, President; Charles A. Atwell, Vice President; Alexander C. Robinson, Treasurer, and Thomas Patterson, Secretary. Five acres of land were leased from Mrs. Robert H. Davis, on Nevin Avenue opposite the ends of Hill and Hopkins Streets and lying between the road and Peebles Run where beautiful old trees and a never failing spring were valuable adjuncts. Walnuts, oaks and sycamores bordered the creek while a group of locust trees out near the ball field furnished shade for the spectators. The new Methodist Church was then being built and the Association was able to secure at a bargain a number of the pews from the old building, which did duty at the Athletic Grounds throughout the life of the organization, accommodating a very wide awake congregation of tennis followers and worshipers of the game. A ball field was laid out and half a dozen courts, afterwards increased to ten or more, with croquet, archery and quoits as additional attractions, and the project was a success from the start. Later, a bowling alley was built on the far side of the creek under the cliff, and for a time it too was quite popular. A modest club house was also erected for the housing of the varied equipment but with no modern country club features. Today it would be mistaken for a chicken house, but it served its purpose. Rackets and balls, as well as nets, were furnished by the club, and only two or three of the more expert players owned "private racquets" with cork handles, as much admired and wondered at as were the new ball-bearing high bicycles. One of those primitive tennis rackets would attract attention in a museum today, with its off-center playing face and general lopsidedness. Though the courts were of clay the game was always given its full title, lawn tennis. Its popularity in this region was just beginning and soon it entirely displaced croquet and archery, becoming a furore among the young and the not-so-young. To read some of the "Lawn Tennis Personals" in *The Qui Vive*, Sewickley's monthly newspaper of that day, is to enjoy a laugh at their naiveté, at the untechnical language in which the sport is described and the extremely personal comments upon the styles of the several players of both sexes. The game was new and the reporting was, to put it mildly, a scream. Nevertheless, some good players were developed and lively games were played, not only between members but with representatives of out-of-town clubs, our particular rival being the tennis club of Brushton, while members of the Sewickley association entering the Western Pennsylvania championship tournaments at Altoona gave an exceedingly good account of themselves.

In charge of the grounds and especially of the tennis courts was "Pa" Gibson, a dour old Scotchman with the richest of native accents, who ruled with a rod of iron and was the terror of any unlucky Junior member who happened to break a racket or damage a net. Ground rules were made to be obeyed, and he was there to enforce them. Woe unto you if thoughtlessly you set foot on a court still wet from recent rains or, worse yet, marred one of his freshly marked lines! Such a torrent of hot Scotch as he would pour on your head! Ride your bicycle off the path and across the corner of a tennis court, and have

"PA" GIBSON

Pa Gibson come hot-foot after you crying, "Hoot mon! Keep on the pad, will ye then!" Never was there a more faithful guardian or a harder working caretaker. Stern-mannered he was, grumbling when you insisted that the rain was over and rackets and balls should be forthcoming, but beneath the grim exterior was a vein of quaint humor that cropped out now and then in a half smile and a twinkle of the eye that belied the outer man and showed that his tyranny was largely assumed, the expression of an intense loyalty to the club, and that in reality he was kind and even soft-hearted. Long will Pa Gibson be remembered.

On the ball field which was laid out nearer the street there was activity, no less than on the courts. Every evening saw pick-up games in progress while intensely exciting matches were played on Saturdays by the Bluestockings, the crack Sewickley nine. Special features on Memorial Day or the Fourth of July were the contests between the married and the single men, but chiefest of all attractions were the Field Days that were held annually; athletic carnivals with a program that included everything in games and sports, field and track events, as well as tennis matches and ball games. One of these is especially remembered which lasted the entire day and was widely heralded as "The County Fair." An admission fee was charged and $1,200.00 realized, a highwater mark in money raising enterprises. One spectacular feature was a quadrille of mounted horsemen, while at the other end of the scale was the climbing of the greased pole by youthful contestants. For the winners in the several events prizes were contributed by the Pittsburgh dealers in sporting goods. In the earlier years of the association the prize winners were content, perforce, with honors only. The prospectus for the season of 1887 announced a series of events in lawn tennis, archery, sprints and high jumps, to continue from May 14th to October 15th, the prizes for which "are the property of the Association awarded to the successful contestants merely as Badges of Honor to be worn until the next Field Day." Strict amateurism, in fact. This conservative policy is readily understood when one considers the extremely moderate annual membership fees that were charged: "Gentlemen $5.00, Ladies $3.00, Juniors $2.00."

THE SEWICKLEY ATHLETIC ASSOCIATION 147

The "Athletic," as the grounds were generally called, was the scene of activities other than competitive games. Picnics, both afternoon and evening affairs, were frequent. Firewood was plentiful and water was supplied by the spring which bubbled up up beside the creek. From the local paper we cull the following: "A social novelty in its way and one likely to possess many features of Hallow E'en joyousness, will be an 'oyster bake' to be partaken of by the young people of Sewickley at the Athletic Club grounds this evening. These beautiful grounds are admirably adapted for such an affair,

AT THE SPRING

and a delightful time is anticipated." Here was the common meeting ground whether for sport or merely for social contacts. While the mornings and afternoons saw the courts well patronized, the evenings brought not only players but great numbers of spectators to enjoy the cool air from the Waterworks ravine and to meet friends and acquaintances. The fences along the street were lined with horses and buggies parked there for the evening, while the newly popular high-wheeled bicycles were grouped here and there on the grounds.

* * * *

It is hard to realize today what a commanding position the Athletic Association occupied in the social life of the town. Nothing else compared with it in popularity. In the winter, entertainments of various kinds were given in Choral Hall to raise money for the coming season, and the opening day each year in May was hailed with delight by all. In the early 'Nineties, due to various causes, the Association declined in popularity, and finally it died out, other interests taking its place, but for over ten years it was far and away the dominating feature of life in the Sewickley Valley.

May, 1928.

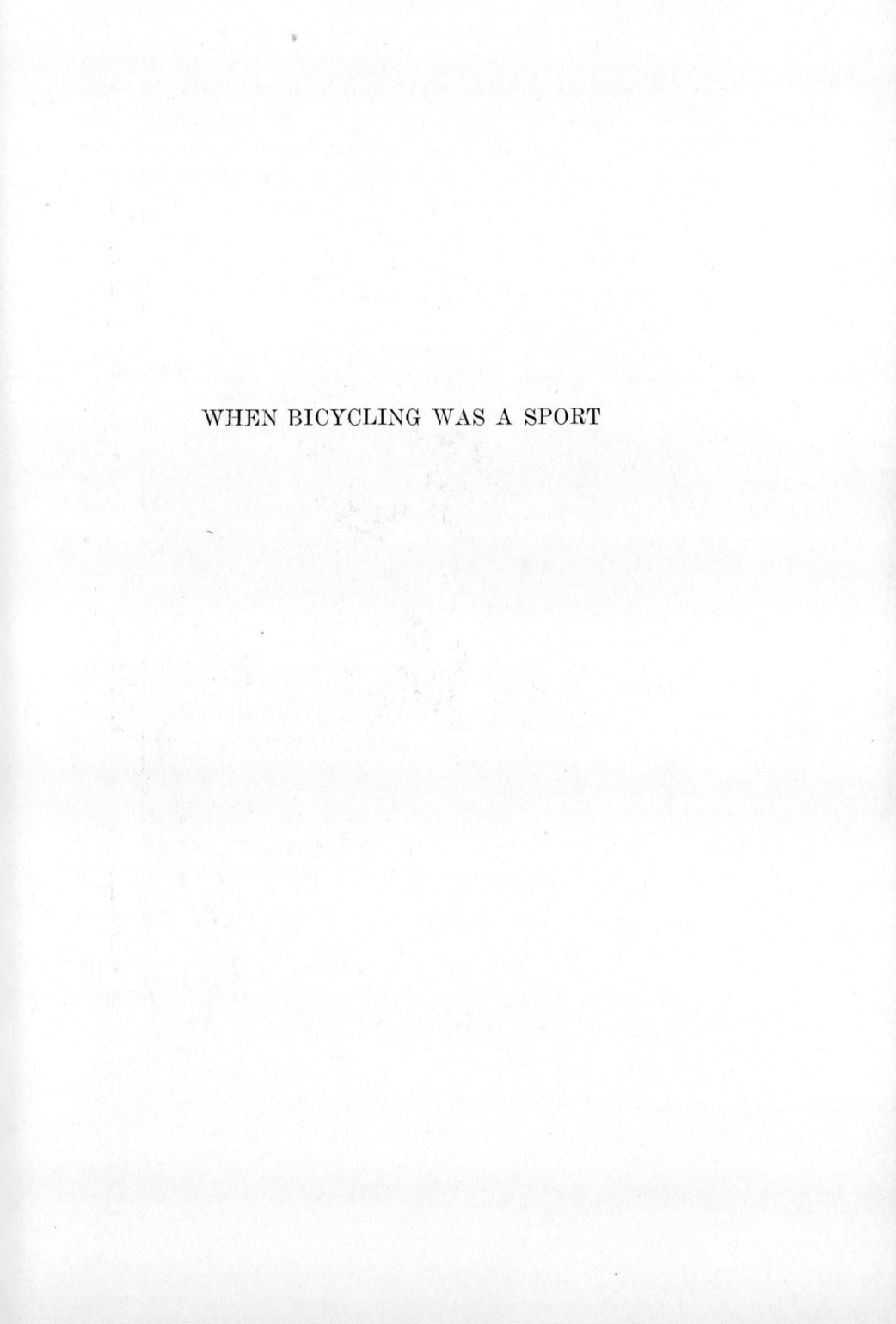

WHEN BICYCLING WAS A SPORT

Charles L. Doyle   E. H. Stowe   F. T. Nevin   M. A. Christy   A. W. Adair
Photographed by J. M. Tate, Jr.

WHEN BICYCLING WAS A SPORT

THE HIGH WHEEL AND THE SEWICKLEY VALLEY WHEELMEN

SEWICKLEY in the 'Seventies boasted of no paved streets. Deep mud and ruts marked the highways in spring and fall, with dust in summer and snow in winter-time. Sidewalks were either of cinders or, at best, of boards laid lengthwise, and prone to warp and turn up at the ends; the "tar walk" had not yet come in nor of course the flagstone pavement. The wooden velocipedes of the very young consequently enjoyed an extremely restricted use, while the few "bone shakers" possessed by some of the more fortunate Sewickley youths in their 'teens barely managed to cruise about town on the sidewalks. These so-called "bone shakers" were large heavy velocipedes with two wheels of equal size having wooden spokes and iron tires, the front wheel equipped with spool-shaped "treadles" and with the saddle swung upon long iron springs between the wheels; a cumbersome and unlovely conveyance; would that one were in existence today, preserved as a curiosity! They were too rough, these "bone shakers," and used up too much power to be really popular even had better roads been available.

* * * *

It was in the early 'Eighties that reports began to come in of a glorified "silent steed" that was making a stir in the East. *Scribner's Monthly Magazine* and *St. Nicholas* carried stories of its growing popularity. "A Wheel Around the Hub," in *Scribner's*, was a fascinating account of a circumnavigating tour about Boston by a party of knickerbockered men riding upon these strange machines that had one wheel as high as the dismounted rider's chin, followed by a diminutive rear wheel at the end of a curved rod or "backbone," both wheels with wire spokes and shod with solid rubber tires.

The *St. Nicholas* article demonstrated that boys could enjoy the new sport as well as their elders.

Then—"came a day" (as the movies say) when a boy stood almost in awe before an exhibit of the Pope Manufacturing Company in the old Exposition building in Allegheny, where for the first time was shown in this region the new vehicle in all its glory of nickeled handlebars, wire spokes like spiders' webs and silent tires of solid rubber. The supreme thrill came when there floated by, as quietly as a ghost, an "Expert Columbia" bicycle ridden by one of the men in charge of the exhibit. The high bicycle had arrived.

Sewickley lost no time in taking up the craze. First one, then another "machine" appeared on its streets, John Warden's the pioneer of them all. Farther and farther afield the riders ventured, contending with dust and ruts and stones; contending too with the other occupants of the highway, horsemen who objected to the new-fangled usurper that frightened their horses and arrogantly claimed to be a vehicle entitled as of right to a share of the road. The sidewalks were no longer available since pedestrians quite rightly objected and moreover the cracks between the boards offered too great a risk of "headers," those sudden unpremeditated dismountings, head first over the handle bars with the little wheel following after to administer the *coup de grace*, a crack on the head, if one failed to dodge it in its descent. Notwithstanding these drawbacks, "Sewickley bicyclists," the local paper said, "are very indignant at the City Fathers because they are compelled by them to direct their fiery steeds through the dust and gravel of the streets."

The number of "wheels" increasing, a bicycle club—The Sewickley Valley Wheelmen—was soon formed, some twenty members enrolled and officers chosen; Seward Murray, President; T. Herbert Nevin, Treasurer, and Robert D. Wilson, Secretary. On the property of Mr. F. L. Clark at the corner of Thorn and Little Streets, under the hill, a modest one-storied club house was built facing Little Street, in plan somewhat resembling a railroad passenger coach with a porch extending throughout its length. Summer evenings saw the club members on the road. Usually they would meet at the Athletic Grounds, then in groups down Beaver Road they would go, and out Little or Big Sewickley creek where the favorite gathering place was at the top of the rise just beyond the Van Cleve chapel. Then toward dusk came the return trip to the club house porch for a smoke and chat and later, lighting the oil lamps that hung from front wheel hubs inside the spokes, the riders wended their several ways homeward.

The new sport was not taken entirely seriously by the general public. Small boys loved to run beside the mounted cyclers shouting "Monkey on a stick," while such facetious comment as the following appeared in print: "A Sewickley Bicycle Club has been organized. Our M. D.'s offices and Chief Justice Rudisill's are putting on a new coat of paint. Broken limbs and runaway teams are expected to make business lively during the dull summer months." Still, the wheel's popularity increased—but not without protest. This semi-serious plaint was voiced on behalf of deserted femininity: "We notice that girls do not take kindly to bicycles and bicycle talk. This can not be wondered at. Every June evening, when the roads are in good condition, there are forlorn damsels sitting alone that would be enjoying masculine attendance but for the silent steed. Three or more girls on an embowered porch and three young men wheeling off in the distance is a sight grown familiar."

Beside these evening excursions, longer trips were taken on Saturday afternoons; most often to Economy where the quiet burghers gazed upon the riders in silent amazement. Among the relics preserved in the Great House is the old hotel register with entries running back to 1849. Search this record through the 'Eighties and you will find registered here and there groups of a dozen or more "Sewickley Valley Wheelmen" who partook of the generous fare of that quaint old hostelry. There we have noted these Wheelmen's names: S. H. Murray, R. D. Wilson, R. C. Swartzwelder, J. C. McKown,

BIG SEWICKLEY BRIDGE—A FAVORITE RESTING-PLACE FOR SEWICKLEY WHEELMEN

A. W. McKown, A. C. Robinson, M. H. McDonald, J. P. Coleman, J. R. Gilmore, F. E. Richardson and R. S. Tate.

Zelienople was visited; and Frankfort Springs was another favorite resort, where the bicyclers sometimes remained over night (and Sundays), or perhaps made the round trip in a single day. Or, the Bluestockings, Sewickley's crack ball team, might have a game on at Brushton, near Wilkinsburg, whither a number of faithful supporters would proceed by wheel, enjoying on their return trip the thrill of coasting down Forbes Street's "Ice House Hill;" that coasting which was the supreme thrill afforded by the high bicycle, as with feet over the handle bars you sat above and almost in front of your rushing steed.

These excursions were events of a Saturday, as has been said. Not yet had Sunday been recognized as a possible day of recreation. After the family carriage had returned from morning service the streets and roads were virtually deserted. Some may remember the half shocked, half puzzled comment when the leader of the Presbyterian choir braved public sentiment by riding his wheel to church of a Sunday morning and parking it against the ivy till the service should be over. Here was food for controversy. He was riding his bicycle on Sunday! Yes—but he was using it solely as a means of getting to church. A puzzling dilemma for the advocates of strict Sabbath observance.

Innovations, new models in bicycles, began to appear. The most radical one was the "Star" which carried its little wheel in front and was equipped with powerful levers, instead of revolving pedals, by which one gained immensely in hill-climbing ability. Then it was that Seward Murray conquered the grade up Murder Lane Road from Beaver Road to the hill-top, thereby setting a hill-climbing mark for all Western Pennsylvania cyclers to shoot at. The fame of that climb spread afar and many came to test their strength and stamina there. The "ordinary" and the "Star" were not long alone in the field. Still newer designs appeared and were tried out.

The Keystone Bicycle Club of Pittsburgh issued an invitation to the wheelmen of Sewickley and other outlying communities to join them on May 30th, 1884, in an all day ride over the old National Pike from Brownsville to Little Washington, a distance of twenty-eight miles, and this brought together a grand assortment of all makes and varieties of wheels. The Standard and Expert Columbia of the Pope Manufacturing Company were the favorite mounts; with the Victor, Star, Royal Mail, Rudge, Kangaroo, Facile, and others in varying popularity. (It might be of interest to note that the fifty inch Expert Columbia cost $127.50, a fair average price.)

The trip to Brownsville was made by steamboat the night before. Next morning appeared the contingents from Uniontown and Greensburg and the entire cavalcade of sixty-seven wheelmen set forth, the hill immediately across the Monongahela furnishing a gruelling test at the very start. A stop was made at Scenery Hill for luncheon and a two hours' rest where the merits of the various wheels were discussed and the incidents and accidents of the morning's ride recounted, while an exhibition of trick riding upon the single front wheel was given by one of the party. Then a blast from the bugle, a hop into the saddle and again we were on our way. At 5:30 P. M. the tourists reached Little Washington where a band of local cyclers and a contingent from Wheeling met them: a street parade followed, composed of "the largest number of wheelmen that ever assembled for touring in Western Pennsylvania."

Among the numerous makes of bicycles which took part in this Decoration Day excursion, one styled the "Kangaroo" calls for special mention. Modelled after the "ordinary" high-wheel bicycle, but in miniature, its pedals were close to the ground and connected with the axle by a sprocket chain. Here for the first time appeared a prophecy of doom for the high wheel, the prototype of the "safety" that was soon to appear, displacing the "ordinary" and casting it upon the scrap heap; that "safety" which was looked upon with scorn as effeminate and lacking in sportiness, but which by its safe riding quality at last completely drove out the old machine. Bicycling remained for some years a real sport. "Century runs" became regular Sunday events as the new wheel proved its worth—but that is another story, coming down into the 'Nineties. With the passing of the high bicycle the gymnastic element in the sport was eliminated and the wheel gradually settled down into its present more or less utilitarian character.

June, 1928.

ROCK SPRING AND THE CAMEL BACK

FROM THE FOOT OF CHESTNUT STREET WE CROSSED TO THE PICNIC PLACE

ROCK SPRING AND THE CAMEL BACK

THE PICNIC PLACE ACROSS THE RIVER

"Rock Spring" and "Camel Back" are unfamiliar names today though once, upon a time long past, they were known to all Sewickleyans; known and visited and loved. Let us leave the automobile at home, to its surprise and chagrin, and set out afoot across the Ohio river bridge to revisit after many years those scenes of former good times. No concrete highway leads to them, so they are necessarily neglected and unknown; thousands of motorists pass along the Narrows Run road at the foot of the hill but seldom or never nowadays does anyone explore the heights above. However, we'll try it. We reach the end of the bridge and, crossing the highway, a steep and impracticable roadway gives us a start up the hill, but soon we abandon it and strike into a narrow foot-path to the right which eventually leads to a spring in the hillside and, just above the spring, to a more or less open space in which are masses of tumbled rocks and some sparse forest trees. Search closely and you may find on rock or smooth-barked beech tree the remains of initials or dates carved there long ago, for this rather forlorn spot was once the picnic ground known as "Rock Spring." There lies the flat rock that served as the table, with other stones about it as seats; there is the open space where always the fire was laid for the boiling of coffee, the frying of bacon and the heating up of the delectable corn pudding. There is the narrow sidling path down to the spring, while just back of the table rock may be seen the beginning of the steep trail that leads to the top of the hill. The spot is readily identified but its beauty has departed, its woods have been despoiled and today it has a mean and sordid look.

Back in the 'Eighties it was not thus. To begin with there was no bridge to make the crossing commonplace. You walked to the foot of Chestnut Street and cupping your hands megaphone-fashion you shouted "O—ver" till the answering cry came back and you saw old Mr. Jolly, the ferryman, shove off and placidly row across to get you. This was Lashell's ferry which landed you at the foot of a path that led past the old log house abandoned long before by the Lashell family for the more modern frame dwelling near by. Both houses are gone now. It was good form to open the gate and go in to ask permission before proceeding up the hill. Across the road and immediately back of the house was the mouth of Lashell's ravine and there began the climb of the steep and narrow trail that we are following in our walk today.

With the river spanned by a great bridge and with our modern means of annihilating distance it is hard to realize the charm that in those earlier days lay in the words "across the river." There was a certain thrill about it as you stepped ashore and sensed the quiet and aloofness of it all; the unspoiled natural beauty, the unfrequented trails, the primitive woodsiness that surrounded you. No wonder is it that Rock Spring was a favorite resort of various picnic groups.

Of one such gathering there is an especially bright recollection. This was known for a number of years as the "Monday Picnic." From early summer till late in the fall no week went by without a meeting of this group which varied in number from a dozen to as many as forty persons. No telephones brought the party together; it was simply an understanding that, weather permitting, the Monday picnic would be held, and if you proceeded to Rock Spring with a basket of eatables you would be certain to meet there with others on similar errand bent. Two o'clock in the afternoon saw the earlier arrivals and five-thirty or six o'clock brought the men from the afternoon train. Supper followed, then all but the few sit-by-the-fires would set out to climb up to the "Camel Back" for an evening view of the valley and a round of songs. Nearing the end of the climb you emerged from the woods onto a grass-grown slope where was a worm-fence and back of it two trees side by side and covered with a thick growth of wild grapevines. One of these trees was taller than the other and together the two as seen from the Sewickley side of the river presented a striking likeness of a camel, which resemblance was helped out by occasional trimmings and prunings. This gave the name "Camel Back" to the entire hill-top. No picnic was complete without a climb to this outlook-point. Then in the gathering dusk the descent to the Spring began where baskets were rounded up, the embers of the camp-fire quenched and, now in total darkness, relieved by the light of a flambeau carried ahead, the descent of the precipitous trail began in single file to the bottom of the hill. To accommodate the entire party the large flat was usually employed on the return trip across the river, and thus another Monday picnic was brought to an end.

The "flambeau" mentioned above was a large ball of kerosene-soaked rags tightly wound, bound with wire and fastened to a pole, the light from which illuminated the woods far around, casting strange shadows but serving materially to make safe the descent. And this calls up the recollection of another illumination that marked an especially eventful gathering of the clan. It was just after the assassination of President Garfield that, as the party sat around the fire after supper, the talk drifted naturally to that all-absorbing topic and each one present exercised his or her ingenuity in devising a horrible punishment for Guiteau, the assassin. The conversational drift in this direction was skillfully managed as a preliminary to the denouement planned by some of the younger members of the party. A life-sized effigy of Guiteau had been fashioned and secretly carried up the hill, where, after dark, it was drenched with oil and hung from a tree limb outside the circle of light. When the last blood-thirsty young woman had outlined her scheme of retribution, one of the party, a young attorney, rose to his feet and in a short speech announced that Guiteau would now be punished on the spot. A light was touched to the figure and the flames shot up revealing a man fully clothed writhing and squirming in the blaze while firecrackers in his pockets and a background of red fire lent horror to the scene. After the more nervously terrified onlookers were restored to calm the affair was voted a shining success, while over in Sewickley the blaze was noted and it was even declared that with opera glasses the figure of a man was seen in the midst of the flames.

The final picnic of the season, in late October, was usually marked by an oyster bake. The struggle to get the half-barrel of shell oysters up the hill was felt to be well worth while as you sat about the fire fishing out of the embers the opening shells and eating the oysters "on the half," piping hot.

The Monday picnics will linger long in the memory of those who were so fortunate as to take part in them and in those memories of by-gone days there will always remain a delightful recollection of "Rock Spring" and the "Camel Back."

September, 1928.

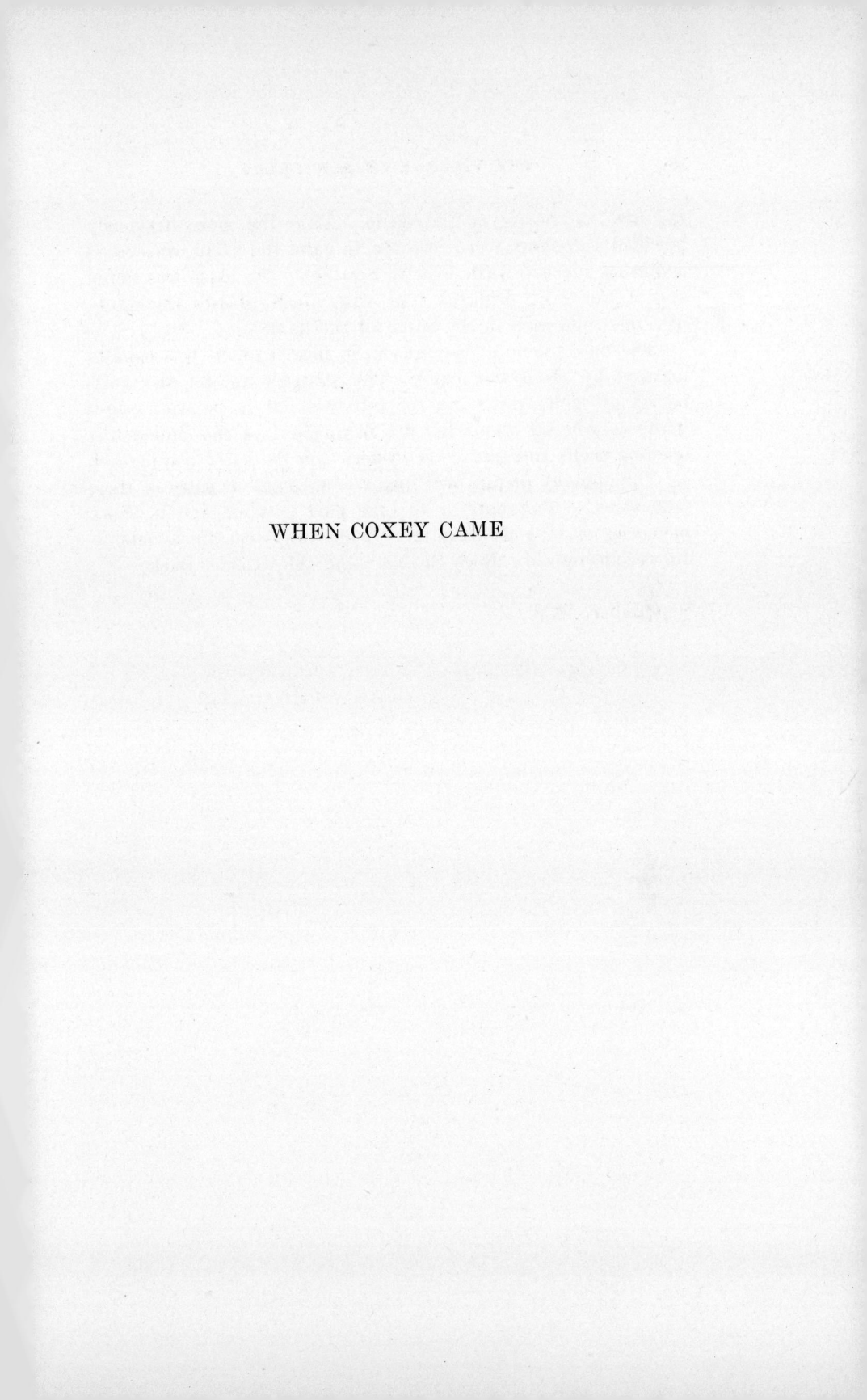

WHEN COXEY CAME

WHEN COXEY CAME

THE ARMY OF THE COMMONWEAL IN SEWICKLEY

SEWICKLEY was somewhat agitated. There were not lacking certain of its citizens who were considerably disturbed. Hidden back of a contemptuous smile there would now and then appear a furtive look of uneasiness. The army that was approaching from the west would arrive in a day or two; who could say what it might not portend? Was it a straw showing the set of the wind, a menace of possible riotous demonstrations against the government? As it rolled on to the east gaining recruits by the way might it not get out of hand and become a frenzied mob bent on storming the capital at Washington, singing some American counterpart of the "Ca Ira" of the French Revolution?

Looking back upon Jacob Coxey's futile gesture from our present standpoint we can afford to smile, recalling his dusty marching Army of the Commonweal and the anticlimax with which it was dispersed upon the capitol steps at Washington. And we smiled—even laughed at it, in the spring of 1894, yet uneasily withal, as not knowing just how serious it might prove to be.

Times were hard and vast numbers of men were out of work. There was a vague demand for legislation which should cure the evils of unemployment. Jacob Coxey of Massillon, Ohio, came forward with a scheme which he believed would remedy the situation. Congress should pass a law permitting each state to issue legal tender certificates to citizens on personal or real property as security, non-interest-bearing bonds, which would ease up the money stringency and result in more work and wages. To bring his ideas before Congress in a dramatic and compelling manner a great Army of the Commonweal, 20,000 strong, would collect from all over the land and march to Washington where Congress, then in session, would be practically forced to heed its demands. A start was to be made from Massillon, recruits to join the Army as it marched along and like a giant snowball, growing as it progressed, it would assume a startling and impressive shape ere its goal should be reached.

One week the Army had been on its way when the Ohio Valley was reached, and while it had been somewhat augmented by hobo recruits and groups of unemployed the marching mob numbered not more than 200 or 300 men and boys. Heavy rains at the start had proved a handicap but now the weather had turned fine and with the warm spring sunshine and the drying up of the roads hope rose high and enthusiasm in the ranks increased. Especially cheering had been the reception accorded the marchers in Beaver Falls, where a warmly enthusiastic crowd applauded the speeches and took up a collection of $50.00 or more to help along the cause, while one of the hotels gave free lodgings to the officers and their mounts. This luxurious over-night rest put so much pep in the leaders that a rather fast pace was set, which resulted in the first appearance of dissension in the ranks. The California commune threatened to split off from the main body. "The Unknown" (and of him, more anon) brought his mesmeric gifts to bear but without success. Finally Marshal Browne brought peace with a promise to set a slower pace—and the march was resumed. The village of Economy was no less cordial than Beaver Falls in its greeting, for Trustee John S. Duss of the Harmony Society had a warm feeling for Coxey, and set about to show that he knew how to treat the weary travellers. Warm and appetizing food was provided in abundance at the Economy camp which Coxey named "Camp Valley Forge," but the ragged army was not made free of the famous old wine cellars of the Society. A wise precaution, undoubtedly. Cheered thus by "the best meal to date," the Army resumed its march towards Pittsburgh on the afternoon of April 2nd, its commander anticipating with something like dread the chilly reception he foresaw upon reaching Sewickley, "the bedroom of Pittsburgh capitalists." And his presentiment proved correct. Passing through Leetsdale the marchers viewed with suspicion and dislike the "magnificent homes'' of the valley residents, while the newspaper correspondents accompanying the cavalcade made much of the contrast between the hobo army and the "gay society people" whose carriages, drags and bicycles crowded the road and who stared with ill-concealed amusement at the dusty marchers. "The terraces of the pretty homes were thronged with sightseers eager to catch a glimpse of Coxey and his army." Whatever may have been their secret feelings there was no appearance of either fear or respect; merely a great curiosity was in evidence. Leading the van, close beside the General and as dusty and bedraggled as the marchers themselves, the reporters came in for comment with the rest. "There go the hoboes. Aren't they the dirty looking people!" There was nothing formidable about the army's appearance, though to make it seem larger the men marched in single file; yet people were puzzled, did not quite know what to make of it. And so, at last, Sewickley was reached.

It was early in the evening that the vanguard topped the rise of Sand Hill and entered the village, where it was planned to spend the night. "General" Coxey himself in a buggy drawn by a white horse was recognized at once. Close on his heels followed the news-writers representing papers in all parts of the country. These occupied vehicles of various and weird description, which were followed by a long line of dusty and bedraggled marchers, the "Army of the Commonweal." Here and there appeared an officer on horseback. Most prominent was picturesque Carl Browne, theosophist and near-anarchist, Coxey's chief of staff, and, riding beside him, the mysterious "Unknown," called also "Unknown Smith," the leader from the far west, whose identity remained a secret to the end. There was "Cyclone" Kirkland, astrologer, meteorologist, "ordnance store officer" and recruiting sergeant; Marshal Broderick of the Chicago commune, in charge of the tents; Iler, the commissary officer, commonly called "Weary Idler" by the correspondents, with his sombrero worn at a rakish tilt; Oklahoma Sam on a wiry western horse with cowboy trappings, galloping about as aide de camp to Browne. And now as the head of the procession is about to enter the town, Jasper Johnson, the standard bearer, climbs out of a buggy, unfurls the American flag and takes his place at the head beside General Coxey, accompanied on one side by his yellow cur dog "Bunker Hill" and on the other, by the half-breed Jackson, long-haired and picturesque, belted with wampum and swinging a big axe. Is it any wonder that Sewickley stared? It was as good as a Wild West show. A lodging for the night was sought and after some dickering and wrangling General Coxey received permission to establish "Camp Duss" on the Grimes lot at the corner of Grimes and Centennial. Here the dusty and weary trampers proceeded to make themselves comfortable for the night, putting up tents, preparing supper and, best of all, resting up. Some of the neighbors were not so comfortable in such close proximity to this motley aggregation but got out their guns and made ready to sell their lives dearly should anybody start anything. Their fears, however, proved unfounded. Nothing happened.

That was a great evening in Sewickley. Everybody turned out to look the Army over; curiosity was not confined to any class. Judge Edwin H. Stowe and Mr. D. C. Herbst innocently stepped over the "dead line" established by the "Unknown" and were unceremoniously hustled out beyond the ropes. When the anarchist was told that he had ejected the President Judge of the Common Pleas Court he said, "I don't care if he is the President Judge of the Supreme Court of the United States. Marshal of Group 19, come forward and put these men out!" This incident was played up in large headlines by the Pittsburgh papers next day: "Bounced a Judge!" There was plenty to see and no lack of excitement, but no real disorder. The sheriff with thirteen deputies and some detectives were on hand, coming from Pittsburgh to have a look-see, expecting to round up some crooks or yegg-men who might attach themselves to Coxey in the hope of gain. They confessed themselves rather astonished to find none of such gentry present. Perhaps the crowd of on-lookers was greatest in front of "Cyclone" Kirkland's astrological chart, listening to his esoteric harangue and asking him to predict tomorrow's weather. The more practical side of his discourse was his recruiting speech, of which the peroration is remembered: "The wives and babies all over this land are crying out for food and the citizens are ready to join in an upraising against the gold bugs and elements on our way and the dawn of the new era is coming."

Carl Browne, Coxey's chief of staff, collected a goodly audience to hear his theosophical speech, ranting about the Reincarnated Christ problem, a speech interesting to some, revolting to others and merely ludicrous to most of those who had the patience to hear him. He harangued the crowd after this fashion: "I address you as fellow dogs and when you hear me out you will not be angry me at me for doing so. We are the dogs, and the monopolists and other capitalists are the fleas sucking away our life blood."

So the evening passed. Gradually the villagers withdrew and Camp Duss settled down for the night, though some twenty weary ones sought more comfortable quarters in the Sewickley lock-up. One desertion from the ranks occurred. It happened in this wise: Mr. William Dickson with the other townsfolk was inspecting the camp, and upon taking a look inside one of the tents he found there a respectable-appearing Scotchman who told a hard-luck tale of unemployment and general discouragement. Mr. Dickson, who had ever a warm spot in his heart for an exiled Scotlander, persuaded the man to abandon the march to Washington and took him to his home where he gave him food, shelter and a job. Next morning the town heaved a sigh of relief as the Army packed up and took to the road again looking forward eagerly to a promised cordial reception in Allegheny and an enthusiastic one in Homestead. Sewickley's chilliness affected not only the rank and file. General Coxey thus unburdened himself to the Pittsburgh newspapers, after speaking of the warmth of Allegheny's greeting: "But what a different reception I got in Sewickley. The people down there are what I term an English snobocracy and are too stingy and niggardly to be classed among decent citizens." Rather peevish of the General, one would say.

Editorially the city papers, while pointing out the futility of Coxey's scheme of legislation, treated him for the most part quite sympathetically, recognizing the man's evident sincerity. And particularly the news-writers and editors laid great emphasis upon the singular freedom from misbehavior and disturbance of any kind, complimenting the Army's leaders for their success in preserving order in camp and upon the march. The worst that was said was that while some of the speeches were a mixture of absurdity and blasphemy and the movement would not be productive of a particle of good to any one and was not an inspiring spectacle, still it was not demonstrably harmful. Sewickley saw it as a Wild West circus and enjoyed the show, once the lurking anxiety as to the "Army's" movements and results was allayed. After thirty-five years General Coxey and his army are still a subject of good-natured comment. The "General" is still living and the people have always had a kindly regard for him as was shown by the popular vote of nearly 53,000 given him when he ran for governor of Ohio the year following his march to Washington; that march which is described as "one of the most remarkable popular uprisings ever witnessed in any country."

January, 1929.

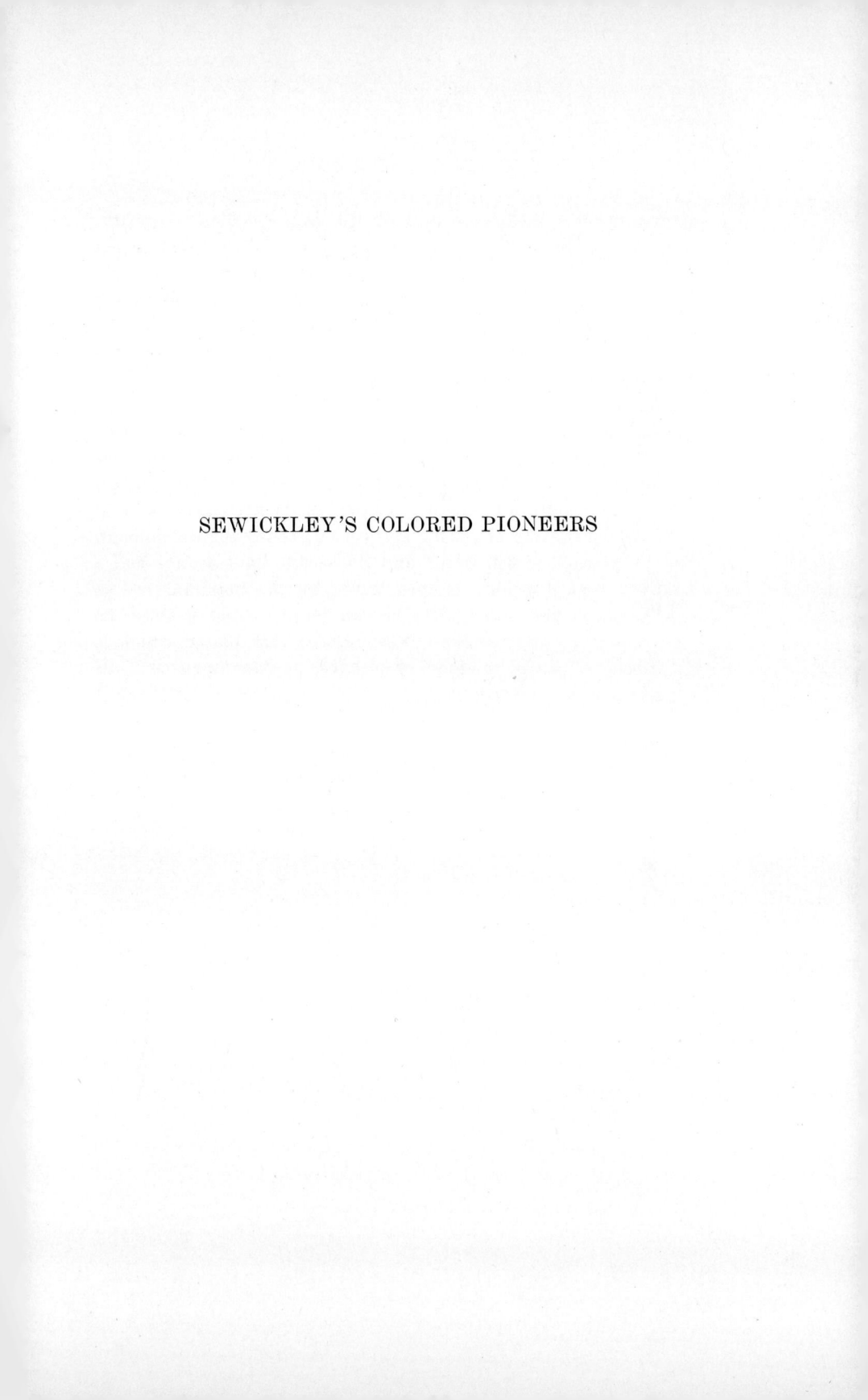

SEWICKLEY'S COLORED PIONEERS

SEWICKLEY'S COLORED PIONEERS

AN APPRECIATION OF THE OLDER GENERATION OF NEGROES

No sketch of old-time Sewickley would approach completeness if it failed to mention the elder generation of colored folk, respected citizens of the village in those days, many of whom are remembered today with a warmth of feeling which is not confined to members of their race, but is shared by the older white inhabitants whose recollections span the years between. Faithful servitors most of them were, in the families of the white folk, the men working in field, garden and barn, the women busy in the kitchen or laundry, and in useful work about the house. Others pushed out into independent lines as small storekeepers, barbers, blacksmiths or as preachers of the gospel. Good folk for the most part they were, conscientious workers and law-abiding citizens, many of them deeply religious, fervent in worship and active in the interests of their church.

Probably the first colored man to come to "Sewickley Bottom," according to Captain David Shields, was one Jim Robinson who was brought as a servant in the Shields household from their former home in Washington County where he had been given his freedom by the Leet family. Washington County, it will be remembered, was a part of Augusta County, Virginia, and hence was slave territory. The Captain remembers Jim as a tall, powerful, black man, famous as a teamster. He it was who laid out most of the roads over the Shields land and drew out logs for the saw mill which, with the Shields grist mill, stood on Little Sewickley creek near where it is crossed by the Beaver Road. Jim was a rugged woodsman. In the winter he insisted on sleeping on the oaken planks of the kitchen in the Shields mansion (now the home of Mrs. Halsey Williams) with his head to the great wood fireplace where it was warmed by the smoldering black gum back-log which Jim was wont to drag into the kitchen with a horse. In Jim's old age the fireplace of the great kitchen was modernized with a stove, and Jim remarked, "It's time fo' Jim to go back to Washington when the Shieldses done got so pore dey got to hab a stove."

In his address on *The Olden Time in Sewickley*, quoted in Miss Ellis's *Lights and Shadows*, John Way, Jr., pays tribute to Mrs. Shields's carriage driver, "a giant African of brawn and muscle, who could neither read nor write, and whose knowledge of mathematics was limited to four,—the number of horses in his farm team. At times, when Mrs. Shields was unable from rheumatism to climb the steep hillside to her little Sunday-school, big Harry Robinson would tenderly assist her with his huge arms. He used his one talent, strength, in a good cause and with a loving heart." (This must have been the *Jim* Robinson of whom Captain Shields speaks.)

Captain Shields has boyhood memories of another old negro, William Blankenship, who was brought to Sewickley Bottom from Ohio by Thomas Shields, "Captain Dave's" father, to serve as nurse for David Shields, the grandfather, in his feeble old age. He remembers how as a small boy he sat with "Uncle Billy" on the fence by the old Shields graveyard to enjoy the novel sight of the railroad train roaring its way to the city at eight or ten miles an hour. Little Dave hugged a fencepost and was held tight by Uncle Billy, following the maternal injunction "not to be sucked in by the train." And how the lad was impressed by Uncle Billy's boast, "I could run one of dem t'ings, Mr. David, if I just knowed how to make it turn de corner!"

In the year 1835 Theodore Nevin, then a youth of twenty, drove a two-horse team from Sewickley to Niles, Michigan Territory, taking with him a black boy "George" to help work the wagon through the "Black Swamp" of Ohio, which lay across their route. The colored lad attracted great attention from the inhabitants along the way, being evidently a rare sight in those parts, and he proved to be lively company on the lonely trip. His master writes: "George is now entertaining mine host and his four sons in the big room. He is caressed at every stopping place; I am asked a thousand different questions about him at every tavern. Last night my landlady's little boys actually quarrelled about getting to sleep with him. The mother being called in to decide the difference, gave the preference to a little white-haired urchin and put them to bed together!''

Not many are living today who remember Franklin Wetzel, generally known as "Old Wetz." Undoubtedly he was one of the earliest of the colored settlers here, for it was on October 3rd, 1865, that he bought from the estate of Catherine Hezlep for the sum of $75.00 a one acre tract lying in what is now the Waterworks Park, whereon he built himself a one-story log cabin which stood on a knoll about where the rustic pavilion is located, a short distance above the lower reservoir. Here he lived for many years though it seems he parted with the title in 1866, selling to his son William Isaac and daughter, Ruth Frances Wetzel, for the astonishing sum of $2,000.00—so at least the deed recites. The son, William Isaac Wetzel, by the way, was for many years in the employ of J. D. Layng of Edgeworth, General Manager of the old Pittsburgh, Fort Wayne and Chicago Railway, acting as porter in charge of that official's special car. They in turn conveyed to the Borough of Sewickley in 1878, the land now forming a part of the waterworks property. "Wetz" was the oldest inhabitant of the valley—of the county in fact, claiming 116 years at the time of his death, which occurred April 3rd, 1879. The *Pittsburgh Telegraph* of the following day honored him with quite an obituary notice on the first page, wherein his birth year is given as 1763, and the statement is made that "his tremendous age is well substantiated and he does not belong to that array of mythical colored patriarchs that contribute to newspaper paragraphs." The notice continues: "In many respects the deceased was a remarkable man both physically and mentally. His bodily vigor was unimpaired by the weight of accumulating years. His memory was something remarkable and at any time he could give a well-connected narrative of events that transpired early in the history of our country." Mr. Franklin Osburn, father of F. C. Osburn, the attorney, carefully questioning the old man, was convinced of the genuineness of his claims. Wetz had come from Charles Town and McPherson's

Mills, Jefferson County, West Virginia, with which region Mr. Osburn, himself a Virginian, was well acquainted, and the old man's accurate and detailed account of persons and places he had known gave evidence of his great age. He told of General George Washington's frequent visits to the home of the Frederick County, Virginia, family where he was a slave, and how he had more than once held the General's horse. In the Centennial year, 1876, Wetz attained a county-wide prominence. A local celebration was staged in Allegheny and the old man was put on exhibition there. He proved a drawing card and the result was the raising of a fund to send him to the Centennial Exposition at Philadelphia, which was successfully accomplished, to his unbounded pride.

They tell of old "Pop" Reese, Charles Reese, who built him a cabin of sod and fence rails up the hollow, beyond Wetz. Later he put up a log cabin on the Jim Winters farm overlooking Little Sewickley creek and near the present site of the Allegheny Country Club, where he worked as a woodchopper. Here he lived through his last years. To him as he lay dying came his pastor, Father Fidler, who discovered that Reese was a former slave whom he, years before, had helped to escape by the "Underground Railroad." Another old-time woodchopper from back in the hills was "Pete" Davis, said to be part Indian. His wife, too, looked as if she had Indian blood as she stalked into the village with long silent strides, her son following behind in Indian file.

It would appear then that even before the end of the Civil War some few colored people had settled hereabouts. When William Curtis, father of David Curtis, came to Sewickley in 1866 he found here a number of pioneers, Franklin Wetzel, George Marlatt, John Howard, Thomas Branson, Israel Jackson, Albert Fields, George Wilson, Sylvester Lee, David Brooks, David Gordon, Albert Seamore, Robert Logan, Dennis Buchanan, William Braxton, William ("Pap") Fisher, Edward Johnson, William and James Parker, Benjamin Ford, Philip Brown, William Henderson and Rev. Billie Fleming. These, with William Warfield, who came in 1868, John Ward, John Pryor, and a few others, may be called the colored pioneers of the valley. Fields was employed by Dr. McCready, Davy Brooks by Mr. Nevin, Seamore by Judge White, Logan by Mr. Murray, Buchanan by Mr. Sands, James Parker by 'Squire Way, Johnson by Mr. Quay, Ford by the Misses Shields, Thomas Branson by Mr. Atwell and Brown by Dr. Dickson.

To attempt a biographical note of each individual would exceed the limits of such a sketch as this, but there was among them an outstanding group, men and women of especial worth, who were marked by dignity of bearing and soundness of character. Concerning these a word of appreciation is due. Of them and some others it can be said that they were of the best quality, scrupulously honest and faithful and in religious matters not given to the emotional extravagance so common among members of their race. There were George Marlatt and "Aunt Callie," his wife. George, tall, heavily built and reputed to have unlimited strength, was a handsome physical specimen, a peaceable, soft-spoken giant. To Rev. Samuel Mackey he related the thrilling tale of his journey on foot from Virginia and over the mountains of Pennsylvania accompanied by his sister, Mrs. Montgomery, and her small son, George, whom he packed on his back the greater part of the way. Reaching Sewickley, Marlatt first worked for Washington Gibb and later he and his wife were for many years in the employ of the Robert H. Davis family. Mr. Davis had bought George's freedom, sending money south for that purpose. "Aunt Callie" was a wonderful nurse and had a wide field of usefulness among the white families about Sewickley, and, later, in Allegheny where she nursed Dr. Louis Willard's patients. George's sister, Mrs. Montgomery, married Dennis Buchanan who worked for Mr. David Sands, while George and his wife lived in a log cabin on the Davis property, close to the site of the present A. J. Barron residence. Here Mr. Davis's daughter Rebekah (afterward Mrs. Dr. Willard) taught both George and Aunt Callie to read and write, and when their church was established she gave to it a handsome pulpit Bible. John Ward, brother of Aunt Callie, and Augusta Ward, his wife, naturally are thought of next. John, clean-cut, dignified and polite, sober in conversation, singularly modest and with high moral standards, was gardener and man of all work for Mr. George H. Christy who in later years secured for him an appointment as messenger in the Federal Courts. He was born, free, in Philadelphia where he grew up and was employed by a German, from whom he learned a few German words which he was fond of using occasionally with an interesting African accent. And Augusta, his wife, the prop and mainstay of all Sewickley's social functions, where she presided in the kitchen and looked after the table appointments as well! Augusta knew as much about correct dinner giving as any white woman in town. The Woman's Club instituted a course of lectures on Domestic Science by an expert from the east, and a number of women subscribed on behalf of their cooks. Augusta was one of those who attended the opening lecture with note-book and pencil. At the close of the session she came to Mrs. Laughlin and showed her note-book untouched, saying, " 'Deed, Mrs. Laughlin, I feel educated—but I got to say I can't read or write." Nevertheless she probably knew more about the art and mystery of cooking than did the lecturer herself. Augusta's first husband had been named Hill, and her son by that marriage, curiously named Murray Hill, was well known in the neighborhood. Some ten years after her marriage to John Ward they gave an elaborate silver wedding party explaining that though she and John had been married but ten years it was the twenty-fifth anniversary of Augusta's first wedding. Poor Augusta, her end was a sad one. Returning from the city one dark night she was killed as she stepped from the train at Sewickley station.

"Aunt Mary" Jackson, sister of Mrs. Marlatt, was another of the members of the group, as was John Howard also, who was a man of some education, a man of parts, with fine manners and a pleasant personality. John, an employee of the old Logan House at Altoona, was brought to Sewickley by Mr. David R. Miller, father of Mr. Chambers Miller. He opened the candy store and barber shop at Chestnut Street crossing, mention of which was made in an earlier paper about "Harbaugh's Pond."

Rather short in stature and inclined to stoutness, with graying hair, he was an amiable kindly man.

William Warfield came to Sewickley from York, Pa., in 1868. He was born, free, in Carroll County, Maryland, and was apprenticed there to a blacksmith. Coming to Sewickley he opened his first shop back of the present Hegner store but later moved to Fife Street (now Blackburn Avenue) back of Dr. McCready's residence. Like John Howard, Warfield was rather stout and of moderate height, a cheerful, good-humored man.

John and Melinda Pryor lived in a little one-story cottage on the edge of what was then known as "The Devil's Half Acre," a name long since discarded as the neighborhood improved. The house stood on Pryor Alley, the only street in the village that is named for a colored man. Self respecting and upright citizens they were; John, tall and rather spare of build; Melinda, quite otherwise. For years John was employed as sexton of the Presbyterian Church where he worshipped with the white folk. Mr. T. H. B. McKnight in a paper read some years ago giving short biographies of the church trustees wrote as follows: "Captain George W. Cochran was elected trustee of the Presbyterian Church in 1873, and held the position of treasurer for twenty years, in which he was ably assisted by the sexton, John Pryor, who attended to the collection of the pew rents, carrying a bunch of already signed receipts about with him, ready for delivery when payment was made. As may be imagined, it was a large and much rumpled bundle to be thumbed over when a pew-holder settled." One of the memorable events in John's life was his presiding at the free lunch which was served on two days in June, 1873, during the auction sale of lots in the Sands and Adair Plan, dispensing hot coffee and ham sandwiches in a barn on the premises. Over $60,000.00 worth of lots were sold at this, the first auction sale of land in the county, and John felt that no small part of the glory was his. When the First National Bank was organized and opened for business, November, 1890, in the "Chamberlin" building across from its present location, John was given the job of messenger which he held to the time of his death. In November, 1894, the bank moved into its present quarters and John pridefully took on all the dignity of a president, cashier and watch-dog combined. Add to this his boast that he was the only colored Democrat in the village, and you realize that John was "different."

Thomas Branson's name belongs in any catalog of Sewickley's colored worthies. "Tommy" was a quiet, modest man, humble in manner, a faithful worker. He and William Braxton were employed by Mr. Theodore Nevin at different times in 1877 and 1878. A pocket memorandum book of those years shows that Tommy was paid $12.00 a month, working in the winter time, while William, employed in the summer, got $15.00. All that they had to do to earn this stipend, besides making garden, picking the vegetables, cutting the grass, helping in with the hay and working generally about the seven acre place, was to care for four horses, five cows and a flock of chickens, and to drive the family to church twice on Sundays and again to Wednesday evening prayer meeting! Still, $15.00 had some purchasing value in those days and the rate of pay was not unusual.

James Parker, a zealous member of the church, was for many years in the employ of "Squire" John Way, looking after the Academy property and premises. William Parker was similarly employed as janitor of the public school buildings. Benjamin Ford, also a pillar of the church, lived "down the road," where he was coachman for the Misses Hannah and Rebecca Shields. Every day he drove up for the mail; his buckwagon and little stylish chestnut horse were familiar to all. A distressing episode in Ben's life was his trial on a charge of murder. The body of a colored girl had been found on the ice pond opposite the Shields residence and suspicion pointed to Ford. His innocence, however, was satisfactorily established and he was acquitted. William Henderson, tall, dignified, with something Indian-like in his bearing, was seldom seen apart from his wagon and white mule. Rev. Daniel Matthews, earliest of the preachers of the gospel, was an earnest and zealous worker, a sincere and godly man. William Curtis, like the bo'sun's mate, "was very sedate yet fond of amusement too," for he and his family coming here from Virginia introduced a somewhat lighter, jollier element. They were full of music and brought with them their plantation songs, the spirituals of today. That musical strain still persists in William Curtis's descendants, some of whom have shown marked talent. The Curtis family, however, did not have a monopoly of musical ability; many others had good voices and enjoyed singing. It is pleasant to relate that it was customary on Christmas eve for a number of the colored men to meet at the home of George Marlatt or John Ward and from there proceed on a round of serenades at the homes of certain of the white folk, where their music and the compliment were greatly appreciated. The story of Curtis's coming is an interesting one; how he was body servant to an officer in the Confederate Army when he broke away, and, with the help of the "Underground Railroad," succeeded in reaching the North and freedom. After a short stay at Duff City he removed to the Murray farm and later to Sewickley.

Lewis Costley, Dr. Allison's driver, lived in the little stone cottage diagonally opposite the Doctor at the northeast corner of Beaver and Academy Avenue, built years before by "Deadman Jim Smith," an old river pilot. George Campbell lived on Captain J. C. Anderson's farm in a little log cabin up the hollow near the present Rea place. Cyrus ("Cy") Bell we all remember, but we may have forgotten that at one time he kept a boarding house on Beaver Street (about where the Mullan store is now, No. 420 Beaver Street), elegantly—or perhaps in derision —known as "Hotel de Bell." Then there was Henry Stafford who worked for the Hays family. He came from near Fredericksburg, Virginia, was body servant to General Alexander Hays, witnessed all the battles down to that of the Wilderness, where the General was killed, and he it was who brought the body home for burial. For many years he remained in the employ of Mrs. Hays at Fair Oaks, Leetsdale and Sewickley. Jacob Portee, brother-in-law of David Curtis, was best known for his violin playing. He was an early addition to the colony. His violin was much in demand at dances and merry-makings. George Montgomery is readily recalled. He was janitor at Choral Hall and an interested on-looker at the social affairs given there. Later he had a job at the court house in Pittsburgh. And so on, and so on. The list could be considerably lengthened but other matters must be recorded.

There was among these old-timers quite a survival of ancient superstition, all trace of which is of course lost today. Odd vestiges of early beliefs, tales of witchcraft and spells, were now and then brought to light in talks around the kitchen fire or between chores in stable or barnyard. White children, the devoted satellites of the old colored folk, were the spell-bound recipients of these confidences. Peter Brooks, before he bought a horse and wagon and went into business for himself, worked as stable man for Dr. Robert McCready. Combing out the snarls in the horse's mane of a morning, Peter told small Robert, Junior, how the witches had ridden the horse that night until it was "all of a lather" and showed the wide-eyed lad the "stirrups" in the horse's mane which the witches had used. Just one way to catch these witches, Peter averred. Place a sieve over the horse's head and the witches couldn't get out till they had counted all of the holes. Then you could catch them. Peter's avocation was preaching. He had quite a local reputation in that line. He was especially gifted in prayer. Once he offered up a supplication for the countless heathen, "thousands, millions—yea *hundreds,* in the world!" Magical cures were more or less popular. If a dog bit you the best treatment was to make a paste containing hair from the dog's back. This spread over the wound was a sure remedy. Now and then would appear in "The Acre" a weird figure reminiscent of southern "voodoo," a large, portly black man displaying snake skins, teeth and various charms, and wearing a necklace of teeth and bones. He was generally spoken of as an herb doctor, claiming to have acquired his knowledge from the Indians among whom he had lived. One of his fearful and wonderful herb concoctions almost did for George Marlatt, who took it internally for a lame knee. The herb doctor's visits were somewhat exciting, accompanied as they were by the laying on of hands and mumbling of incantations over bear's teeth and charms, but his voodoo was a bit too crude to obtain much of a following among the Sewickley negroes. Belief in a personal devil who masqueraded in various disguises was quite common. "Granny" Curtis, a famous cook in the Davis family, coming to work in the early morning, meets a black dog on the way and recognizes it as His Satanic Majesty on some baleful errand bent. Ghost stories were a favorite entertainment. On holidays groups of colored folk would meet and spend the entire day reciting these thrilling tales and singing their southern melodies. Some little drinking marked these occasions, the favorite tipple, eggnogg, but it can truthfully be said that there was no drunkenness there—and rarely any dancing, for dancing was frowned upon by the sedate elders.

Some account should be given of the colored people's religious activities. Mention has been made in a former paper of the Sunday afternoon bush meetings held in Mr. J. Sharp McDonald's grove, those open-air revivalistic assemblies where the natural religious exuberance of the race was given full swing. These meetings were a late survival, for back in the 'Sixties there had been a series of such gatherings in what was known as "Linn's Hollow," now the Waterworks Park. These were all-day Sunday affairs, several of which would be held in the course of a summer season. In the 'Sixties also and repeated during two or three years, there was an organized camp meeting in McKown's grove, on the river bank at Glen Osborne station. These meetings were attended by colored folk from far around. Tents were put up and the services lasted ten days or longer, presided over by two bishops, the one a typical southern negro orator named Moore, the other, Bishop Jones, a man of better education and more polished manner. Certain of the local citizens were prominent at these meetings, John Howard, Franklin Wetzel, William Henderson and others. But, earlier even than the camp meetings in McKown's grove, in 1857 in fact, the Rev. Daniel Matthews, an earnest and enthusiastic worker for souls, had established a colored mission in Sewickley which held services in a log building located near what is now the corner of

Broad and Centennial, and later in another log building on Walnut Street, next to the present Catholic church. George Marlatt's family occupied the rear portion of the building. It was about the year 1868 that John Howard, Wetz, Warfield and a few others approached Mr. Theodore Nevin with the request that the white people help in founding a colored church in the village. Mr. Nevin and Judge White consented to act as trustees of a fund to be collected for the purpose, and the church was formally established, taking the name of St. Matthew's A. M. E. Zion, as much in honor of the Rev. Daniel Matthews, it is said, as of the evangelist of that name. Years of varying fortune followed; years of discouragement and apparent defeat followed by times of enthusiasm and prosperity. The lot at the corner of Thorn and Walnut was purchased and the frame church built which was later moved back to make room for the present brick building. In the 1880's Mr. George H. Christy presented to them a small frame house which was moved from the Christy lot to its present location facing Thorn Street where it is used as the parsonage. Then, in the year 1903, a church charter was secured, the present writer having the privilege of preparing and presenting in court the petition which was signed by John P. Ward, John Burnard, David S. Curtis, William Mossett, T. E. Hines, Jefferson Granison, James Parker, Mary Johnson and Lucy Carter, the first five being named as trustees. The matter came up before Judge Collier in old Common Pleas Court No. 1. His Honor slowly read over the full name, "Saint—Matthews—African—Methodist—Episcopal—Zion—Church—of—Sewickley—Pennsylvania," and asked, "Are you certain that you have the whole name there?"

It is not proposed here to write a church history. Suffice it to say that with varying fortunes, some internal disturbances and defections, and under many pastorates, certain ones marked, as was the Rev. Durham's, by a pronounced success in raising funds, the church continued to advance, and in the year 1917 at its 60th year celebration, the mortgage was burned amid great rejoicing. The A. M. E. Zion is the pioneer church for colored people in the valley. Others followed later but being more modern they are not properly to be included in a sketch of the olden times.

Like their white neighbors the colored folk found in their church organizations a favorite field for social as well as religious activities. Church bazaars and strawberry-and-ice-cream festivals were not uncommon or unusual events, but one entertainment that was given by the younger element on a certain summer afternoon in the mid-'Seventies, long stood as a high-water mark in the annals of Sewickley's colored population. This was the "Tournament of the Knights of the Red Cross" held on the Sands and Adair lots fronting on Frederick Avenue between Walnut and Little Streets. Twenty young fellows from Sewickley with ten more from Bellevue were organized and drilled by Prof. Neal, a colored school teacher from Allegheny. The tilt-yard extended along Frederick Avenue with a flag and bunting-draped arch erected opposite the residence of Mrs. General Hays. From the center of the arch hung a ring at which the riders stabbed with their tin-pointed lances as they galloped past to the rattle of drums and the blare of trumpets. The spectators crowded close to the lists cheering the several riders, while the judges' stand and Mrs. Hays's porch were filled with an applauding audience. The prize went to the Knight who collected the greatest number of rings on his lance and he it was who won the honor of crowning as queen the dusky beauty of his choice. Alex Warfield, now a county employee in the office of the Prothonotary, was chief marshal, mounted on Mr. J. Sharp McDonald's "Kate," the ancient white mare celebrated as the oldest equine in the valley. (Forty-four years she numbered when she died.) There was George Montgomery riding Dr. McCready's roan "Kit," full of pep and bounce; Charlies Gilkerson mounted on "Dolly Varden," and Beverly Gilkerson, William Braxton, Tom and Jim ("Quickstep") Matthews also ran. The prize went to Ed Johnson on Col. McKelvy's army mare, "Sis Lee" and he it was who crowned Eva Mason as the "Queen of the Tourney."

This brings us to the younger generation of near-old-timers, Charlie and "Bev" Gilkerson, George Ward and others. Feelings of genuine respect coupled with pleasant memories come over one in recalling the kindly and in some ways child-like old colored folk. It is not with respect so much as with amusement that some of the younger negroes are remembered, George Ward, for instance; nephew of John, who brought him up, a mischievous sky-larking, banjo-playing fellow who tried but never seemed to break the patience of "Uncle John." Long, lank and preternaturally solemn-looking George was, with a bass voice that came up from his boots, verily from the heels thereof. Any employment that was not too steady suited George. For instance when the perennial Sewickley Minstrels were booked for a performance in Choral Hall George was hired to advertise the event. All day he paraded the streets in long-tailed coat and slouch hat with an old-fashioned musket on his shoulder, and on his back a sign reading "I'm looking for the Man Who Is Not Going to the Minstrels Tonight." Death came to George while he was yet a young man. Shortly before he passed away his minister called at his bedside and asked, "George, are you prepared to die?" George replied, "Yass sir. Pretty ready. I got a first rate coat, but my pants ain't jest what they'd ought to be." And "Betty" Harris—who remembers Betty Harris, George's partner in various escapades? For "Betty" was a boy, strangely misnamed, and fully as mischievous as George. Betty, George and "Fling" Henderson formed a trio that was hard to beat. Then there were the Gilkersons, Charlie, Beverly and Ed, whose steadiest employment was at housecleaning time—though Beverly long worked for Mrs. Hutchinson and brought up a family in the building in Mrs. Hutchinson's yard which is now the office of Doctors Nettleton and Mitchell. Charlie Gilkerson's passion was debating. Many a hilarious gathering in the A. M. E. Zion Church applauded his oratory as he pounded the pulpit and pressed home his arguments to prove that "Steam power is more valuable than horse power" or to decide "Which is the most beautiful to the eye—art or nature?" It was a bold man that challenged Charlie to debate. Even Ajax Jones, the colored orator and politician from Pittsburgh, met his match in this forum. At the height of his oratory Charlie's cuffs would work out of his sleeves and over the ends of his fingers, falling to the floor in front of the pulpit when he reached his peroration. And his peroration was well prepared, for Charlie, to prime himself for the occasion, would go down to the Academy and get the boys to give him some "good words" to use. It didn't matter what they meant "just so they sound good" he would say. Crowded assemblies attended these contests, the judges always chosen from among the white folk present.

Lively tales could be told of the younger colored element typified by George Ward and Charlie Gilkerson but when we look back across the years and recall those pioneers of the colored race who made their homes in this valley in the days immediately following the Civil War—their War of Independence; when we consider their sterling qualities, their honest and God-fearing lives, their fidelity in humble employment—then we believe that the present generation cannot fail to realize that there has been handed down to them a precious heritage, a fine tradition and an example which they and their children's children should preserve and cherish.

January, 1929.

* * *

For valued assistance in the preparation of this paper acknowledgment must be made to Captain David Shields, Messrs. Gilbert A. Hays, Robert T. M. McCready, Bayard H. Christy, F. C. Osburn, Rev. Samuel Mackey, David S. Curtis and Alexander Warfield.

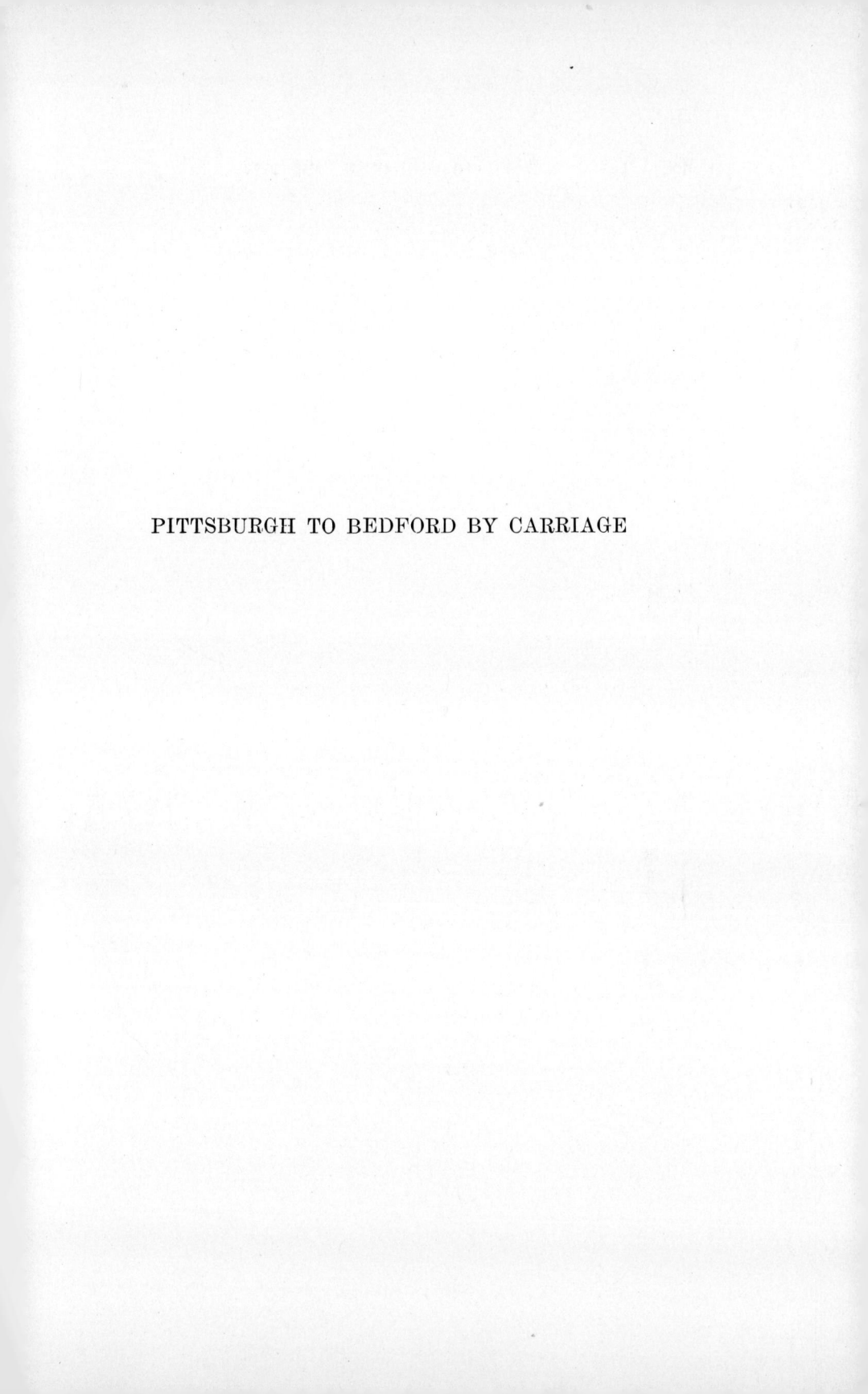

PITTSBURGH TO BEDFORD BY CARRIAGE

PITTSBURGH TO BEDFORD BY CARRIAGE

FROM A BOY'S DIARY OF 1878

BEDFORD, Pennsylvania, is on the Lincoln Highway—formerly the Philadelphia turnpike—100 miles east of Pittsburgh. The modern motorist who does not "make" it in three hours, or less, thinks he is wasting time on the road. The following extracts from a boy's diary of fifty years ago give an impression of travel over the turnpike in that day, a glimpse of a more placid form of enjoyment, with an appreciation of the amenities of the highway such as is scarcely the vogue today; a journey in which the three days seemed all too short.

It is thought that this small-boy chronicle might not inappropriately be included among such a collection of papers as this, as showing something of the same simple pleasure as was characteristic of life in the Village of that day.

* * * *

Monday, Sept. 2, 1878

This morning Dave (who is my best friend) and I were up in our carpenter-shop that we have over the cow stable working on a printing press that we are making when Sister Lide called me and when I went into the house she told me that Father says I can go with them tomorrow on a trip to Bedford Springs in the carriage. Father, Cousin Fanny, Sister Lide and I are going. My but I was glad and excited for I rode to Bedford Springs with Father once before and I know what fun it is. I am going to keep a diary this time and put down everything. Sister Lide helped me to pack my valise this evening because Mother is not at home. She is at Bedford Springs with Cousin Mary, waiting for us. This afternoon William Braxton our colored hired man hitched up the two horses and drove up to Allegheny so we can start from there tomorrow morning early.

Tuesday, Sept. 3, 1878.

This morning Father, Sister Lide, Cousin Fanny and I came up to town on the 1/4 to 8 train and after I got my hair cut we waited a little while in Father's office at the bank and then the carriage came and we all got in and started at 10 A. M. The two horses, Dick and Sam, were as anxious to start as we were and could hardly wait for us to get in. Dick Swiveler and Sam Weller are their full names; Father says in honor of Mr. Charles Dickens. All the men in the bank stopped work and came to the door to see us off and we went with a hurrah, down Federal Street and across the "Suspension Bridge" to Pittsburgh. My but the streets were full of wagons, carriages and horse cars. It took us a good while to drive out Penn Avenue to Wilkinsburg where at last we were on the Greensburg turnpike. We had to pay a toll almost as soon as the pike began and I have decided to keep track of the number of toll-gates and the amount we have to pay; it was ten cents this first time. We are now at Turtle Creek for lunch. We got here at 12 M. and had a splendid drive.

This afternoon we drove to Mt. Pleasant; it took us till 7 P. M. We thought that from Pittsburgh to Mt. Pleasant was 33 miles but we found to our suprise that it was 40! We haven't tackled the mts. yet. We are at the Jordan House at Mt. Pleasant. We paid 33c toll today.

Wednesday, Sept. 4, 1878.

Joneses Mills. We got down to breakfast after having a very pleasant night. Sister Lide and Cousin Fanny's room and Father's and mine were adjoining and right on the street. We came mighty near being caught in an awful thunder storm last night. Dick was overcome with the heat and he would not eat anything. This morn we were not quite sure whether he could stand the drive to Somerset (28 miles) from Mt. Pleasant. But he is all right now. We are stopping at Joneses Mills for dinner. I forgot to say that we passed through Madison yesterday. We all walked up Chestnut Ridge except Cousin Fanny and she drove. I am just through dinner and so is Father. There goes Father out to see about the horses and we will start in a minute. I carved my name on the rail of the porch and wrote Dave's with a lead pencil. We left Mt. Pleasant at 8 A. M. and got here at 12 M., noon, 12 miles. We drove slowly on Dick's account. It is 17 miles to Somerset from here and we want to get there by night.

We got here (Somerset) at 1/2 past 6. We have had a splendid drive. We rode over Laurel Hill just after leaving Jones Mills. My but the mountains are lovely. We got lots of mountain tea. The horses walked the whole way and it took an awful long time. We all took turns walking too to help the horses. A man on the road who had just walked over the mountain said "It's a long pull. Better rest your horses now and again." Father said Yes he knew the mountain well. I drove part of the time and the rest got to the top before the horses and I did. Cousin Fanny picked a lot of wild flowers and they made the carriage look real pretty. We are at the Somerset House. This is a good hotel. We have got real nice rooms. We are going to get up and start early tomorrow for we have 38 miles to travel. We have gone 28 miles today. We paid no toll today. We left Mt. Pleasant at 8 R. M., and got to Somerset at 1/2 past 6.

Bedford Springs, Thursday, Sept. 5, 1878.

We got breakfast and started at 20 min. after 7 A. M. Dick's 'most all right now but neither he nor Sam are eating much. We rode 21 of the most beautiful miles there are over the mts. to a little hamlet called West End where we ate lunch. We had only 17 more miles to Bedford and so we made it easily. We left the turnpike at West End and took a road along the "blue Juniata." My finger that was sore is 'most well and healing up rapidly. We had one of the lovelyst views from one of the Alleghenys that is anywhere to be seen. O My! but it was bee-autiful! We crossed two or three mountains today. We got on the pike again at Man's Choice and I got a fearful headache which lasted till I got here at Bedford. My but it did ache. Father said to a young woman What place is this and she said Man's Choice. Father said she looked embarased. We arrived here at a little after seven and drove to the Arandale Hotel. The people were all out on the porch when we got there and we were pretty dusty and dirty. Mother and Cousin Mary were there and said they were very well. And now the first part of the trip is ended. Golly but it was fun. We are going to stay here a week and then drive home again. First day 40 miles, 2d day 28 miles, 3d day 40 miles, 108 miles altogether. We paid 43c toll.

* * * *

Monday, Sept. 9, 1878.

Today we started home again and I am going to write in my diary again because we are going back a different way. My but Sam and Dick are skittish after resting all week! Father says the Bedford Springs water seems to have done them good. They like the iron water too. It is so strong I don't like it much. The sulphur water is awful bad. We started from the Arandale at 1/2 past 7 A. M. We had a real nice ride. This time we are going over the turnpike that runs from Philadelphia to Pittsburgh. We stopped at the Stoy House on top of the mountain for dinner, 19 miles. After dinner we had an awful rough ride. It was foggy when we reached the top of Allegheny mountain and Father said we were driving in a cloud. We were so high up it was a cloud. On the way up it cleared so we had a magnificent view over the valley and saw the farms below. Father stopped the horses one place and had a talk with a farmer working in a field. He let the horses heads down and they nibbled the grass at the side of the road. Father told the man how he had worked on his father's farm near Shippensburg when he was a boy. They had a good talk. I remembered the barn at the Stoy House where we stopped when I rode over with Father and Uncle Daniel and my sister Mary. That was three years ago and I went to the barn with the hotel keeper's boy to see some new baby pigs and Father pretended to drive off without me. I ran and caught up and pretty near cried. I was a baby then. This afternoon we drove to here. It is 38 miles from Bedford Springs. We are stopping at Judge Pickings now at Jenners Cross Roads at the foot of Laurel Hill. We paid 37c toll. The road is awful rough and when we pay toll Father most always tells the toll-gate keeper that he ought to pay us instead of us paying him. Father says the pike used to be kept in good shape when the stage coaches ran but now no one hardly uses it any more. We had two jokes on Father today. Once when we stopped at a spring to a get a drink he said Wait till I open my valise and get out my drinking cup. While he was hunting for the cup a pistol dropped out and we all laughed and asked him how he expected to protect us with the pistol in the valise packed under the front seat. He just laughed too. Then Cousin Fanny thought she had a good joke on Father when she saw a paper covered book called That Beautiful Wretch sticking out from under his shirts in the valise. O Well was all Father said. He didn't care and laughed. We went through Shellsburg and Stoystown today. The pike is awful steep through Stoystown. But the principal part I liked was the long straight stretch where you can see the road ahead of you for I guess over six miles. Anyhow it took us over an hour to get from one end of it to the other. Then we stopped the horses and looked back to see where we had come from. I am awful tired and sleepy.

Tuesday, September 10, 1878.

We all had a boss sleep and a bosser breakfast. Father is helping a man hitch up the horses and we are going to start pretty soon so I'll write some more in my diary. I'll have to copy it in ink when I get home. This is an old log house and Father has known Judge Picking a long time. He doesn't look much like a judge we said but I guess he was one once. Father says he was one of those judges who never were lawyers but just judged by their common sense. I slept with Father in one room and Cousin Fanny and Sister Lide were in the room across the hall. It was awful funny going upstairs to bed because the stairs leaned in and you had to hold on to the bannisters. Cousin Fanny said it was like the Leaning Tower in Italy. I forgot to tell about how our wheels rattled before we got here. The spokes of the wheels were loose so last night Father took off all four of them and laid them in the creek to soak and this morning they are "as tight as wax" he said. Now the carriage is ready.

We started from Judge Picking's at 20 min. to 8 A. M. We went right over Laurel Hill but Father forgot to get the wheels greased so we found a stick and greased them ourselves. We drove through Ligonier and Father said he would have to taste the beer they make here. And so he did at the hotel. It is made by the monks or something at a place called St. Vincents. [St. Vincent College, Latrobe.—*Ed.*] We are stopping for dinner at the Union House at Youngstown. We hadn't a good dinner at all. We will try to make Turtle Creek for the night. We have traveled 14 or 15 miles. The owner of this house has 22 children. He married one of two sisters and had 10 children, another man took the other sister and had 7. This hotel keeper's wife died and so did the husband of the other sister. The two left were married and had five children, $10 + 7 + 5 = 22$! Most all of the first are in California. I didn't eat any of the miserable dinner. We started at 10 min. after 2 P. M. Thunder! But the sun was hot. But it cooled down soon. We had a beautiful ride all day and did 36 miles from Judge Pickings to here at Jacktown and paid 52c toll. Horses all right. My but the road down Laurel Hill is long. We most all walked part of the way up and part of the way down. About half way down there is an old tavern beside a big bend in the road. Father turned Dick and Sam in to take a drink at the watering trough. Golly but they were glad. It was fun to see them stick their faces into the water clear up to their eyes almost and snort. This afternoon I saw something that I remembered. It was on a big stone in front of a farm house and said Root Hog or Die. I remembered it and so did Father and he said a farm is no place for a loafer. Out beyond Greensburg we were talking with a man who said we ought to drive off a mile or two and see a burning spring. So we did and the road was not so bad as the pike. Father said he had heard of the burning spring and would like to see it. It really was on fire and looked awful queer. It came up through the water in bubbles and some one had lighted it with a match. It has something to do with the petrolium that there is in the ground. Father said that he and some other men bored a well not far from there in 1858 looking for oil but didn't find any. The well was 400 feet deep. We started from Judge Pickings at 1/2 past 7 A. M., and got here at the McIntyre House in Jacktown at 7 P. M. We drove by moonlight. This is a boss little tavern.

Wednesday, September 11, 1878

Had a splendid breakfast at 6 A. M. My, I never tasted anything so good. Chickens, waffles, honey, beefsteak and hosts of other things. Golly but it was good! Started at 1/2 past 6 A. M. and passed through Turtle Creek and arrived in Allegheny at 11 A. M. We went right through down to old Sewickley and got here at 10 min. of 1 P. M. The horses are fresh as when we began the trip. Rode 37 miles today. Paid 18c toll. First day, 38 miles; 2d day, 36 miles; 3d day, 37 miles—altogether 111 miles. We paid 43c toll going and $1.37 coming back. We got some brown biscuits for lunch. They were not expecting us till late in the evening and we suprised them mightily. We have just missed Barnum's Circus. I went over to see Dave and he and I and the rest went in swimming.

LORETTO AND ALEPPO

LORETTO AND ALEPPO

SOME ACCOUNT OF THE EARLY LAND TITLES IN SEWICKLEY

THE following notes were taken from the records in the offices of the County Engineer, the Recorder of Deeds and the Register of Wills of Allegheny County, in running the chain of title to the land now occupied by the Sewickley High School. They are of interest as showing the origin of Sewickley land titles in general.

* * * *

Allegheny County was erected from parts of Washington and Westmoreland Counties in 1788, and in 1792 there was added to it the triangle on Lake Erie purchased from the United States. Originally the county was divided into five townships, of which one called Pitt embraced all the land lying north and west of the Ohio and Allegheny rivers and extending to Lake Erie. In 1796 Pine township was cut out of Pitt, and in 1800 the county was reduced to its present size by the creation of Armstrong, Beaver, Butler, Crawford, Erie, Mercer, Venango and Warren counties. In 1803 followed the creation, from a part of Pine, of a new township named Ohio, within which, in 1853, was erected the borough of Sewickley.

Division Street within the borough marks a portion of an almost exactly north-and-south line dividing two districts of the Depreciation Lands, which were surveyed respectively by Daniel Leet and Nathaniel Breading, two of the Deputy Surveyors of the State.

The tract lying immediately west of Division Street was the farm *Loretto*, which was surveyed by Daniel Leet in the month of April, 1785, in pursuance to instructions from the Surveyor General dated the second day of January, 1785. It was Lot No. 1 of District No. 2, and contained two hundred fifty (250) acres with the usual allowance of 6 per cent for roads. The property was purchased by Levi Hollingsworth when the lands were put up for sale at the English Coffee House on High (now Market) Street, Philadelphia, but was released by him to Mark Wilcox, to whom the patent was issued. Returned the eleventh of January, 1786, to Mark Wilcox. Patent Book P-5-119. These patents are enrolled in the Rolls Office at Harrisburg, where they can be seen and examined. Mark Wilcox and Mary, his wife, by deed dated December 6, 1786, sold *Loretto* to Jonathan Leet (Deed Book vol. 2, page 469, in the office of the Recorder of Deeds for Allegheny County). Consideration, 62 pounds. Jonathan Leet and his wife, Mary, sold to Henry Ulery, April 10, 1798 (D. B. vol. 8, page 111), consideration, 98 pounds, 15 shillings. That deed contains the following which is all that our county records show back of that date: "Which said Tract of land (250 acres) was surveyed by Daniel Leet, one of the Deputy Surveyors of District No. 2 within the Tract of land appropriated for the redemption of the Depreciation Certificates by an Act of Assembly passed the 12th day of March 1783, entitled an Act for the Sale of certain lands therein mentioned for the purpose of redeeming and paying off the certificates of Depreciation given to the Officers and Soldiers of the Pennsylvania line and which said described Tract is marked in the survey and plan of the said District 'No. One' and was sold to Levi Hollingsworth at Public Auction being the highest bidder, who released the same to Mark Wilcox to whom the Patent was issued bearing date the 19th day of January 1786, who conveyed the same to Jonathan Leet by deed dated the 6th day of December 1786. Reference thereunto will more fully and at large appear."

Henry Ulery sold *Loretto* to Thomas Hoey October 22, 1814 (D. B. vol. 20, page 72), consideration $4,000.00. Thomas Hoey, for $4,000.00, sold part of the farm "to Charles and Sophronia Thorn and their children and assigns" on April 7, 1828 (D. B. vol. 36, page 293—corrected in D. B. vol. 97, page 30). This property ran down to the Ohio River and was that part of *Loretto* farm whereon Rev. Charles Thorn and his wife, who was the daughter of Thomas Hoey, resided. The children were Mary and Sophia, minors, who afterwards married Judge J. W. F. White and William Harbaugh. The peculiar form of this deed which was "to Charles and Sophronia Thorn and their children and assigns" made necessary certain court proceedings, at No. 54 March Term, 1839, with deeds back and forth (James Chadwick taking title between-times) and finally a deed of partition whereby J. W. F. White and Mary E. White, his wife, on December 2nd, 1852, conveyed to Sophia E. Harbaugh, Mary's sister, the piece above the railroad containing four acres, 37.78 perches; and on July 26th, 1853, William Harbaugh and Sophia, his wife, sold it to David N. White for $1,694.45 (D. B. vol. 110, pages 105-108). (Rev. Charles Thorn lived till June 30, 1874. Will dated March 21, 1874, Will Book 17, page 520.)

The tract lying east of Division Street was called *Aleppo*. It contained 234 acres, 91 perches, and was Lot No. 126 of District No. 3, which was allotted to Henry Pratt of Philadelphia and was surveyed by Nathaniel Breading June 26, 1875, pursuant to instructions from John Lukens, Esquire, Surveyor General, dated at Philadelphia the 5th day of March, 1785. Patent Book P-5-46. What Henry Pratt paid for the patent does not appear—though of course he paid in Depreciation Certificates on a gold basis.

On September 7th, 1793, Henry and Elizabeth Pratt sold *Aleppo* to Jonathan Leet (D. B. vol. 5, page 233) for 70 pounds, 7 shillings and 6 pence. Between that date and April 10, 1798, a period of five years, when he sold *Loretto* to Henry Ulery, Jonathan Leet was the owner of the combined tracts *Aleppo* and *Loretto*, 484 acres, 91 perches, at a total cost to him of 132 pounds 7 shillings, approximately $643.00. Jonathan and Mary Leet on April 7th, 1802, sold *Aleppo* to John Vail (D. B. vol. 11, page 411) for 233 pounds. John Vail and Sarah, his wife, parted with the title the same day for $1,752.00 to Thomas Beer (D. B. vol. 11, page 57). Beer died leaving a widow and nine children, all of whom joined in a deed to Samuel and Robert Peebles, April 24, 1834; consideration $4,400.00 (D. B. vol. 51, page 447).

On the death of Samuel Peebles his share in *Aleppo* was by his last will and testament (Will Book 4, page 319) devised to his executor, John Graham, to whom Robert Peebles by deed dated December 15th, 1842 (D. B. vol. 75, page 506), conveyed his half interest also, and John Graham by deed dated November 1st, 1848 (D. B. vol. 83, page 186) for a consideration of $5,100, conveyed to Robert Hopkins 50 acres between the Beaver Road and the Ohio River. (Also 64 acres north of Beaver Road.)

Rev. Robert Hopkins and Pamelia, his wife, by deed dated February 21st, 1854 (D. B. vol. 111, page 360), conveyed to David N. White the plot bounded by White's property (acquired from the Harbaughs) and by Harbaugh, Graham and Railroad Streets. Robert Hopkins's deed also passed such title as he might have in the old graveyard which Beer and Ulery had set apart at the foot of Division Street—or "Graveyard Lane."

David N. White ("Deacon" White) now owned a combined piece of property lying across the line that divided *Aleppo* from *Loretto*. He and his wife, Dianna, on May 3rd, 1858 (D. B. vol. 146, page 391), sold the whole tract, five acres more or less, to Griswold E. Warner for $9,100.00. Following the death of "Judge" Warner the two pieces were again separated. His executors, Franklin Osburn and D. N. White, on May 15th, 1873, under a power contained in his will (Will Book 16, page 389), sold to Harriet A. Gilmore, for $15,000.00, (D. B. vol. 306, page 332) the piece since known as the Gilmore property, and by Articles of Agreement dated May 15, 1873, confirmed to Henrietta W. Osburn, "Judge" Warner's daughter, the piece across the line in *Aleppo* since known as the Osburn property (D. B. vol. 318, page 9). This was done in accordance with a provision in her father's will.

Partition proceedings were necessary in Orphans' Court, at No. 4, December Term, 1889, to confirm title in the Osburn heirs, with another deed by Franklin Osburn, Surviving Executor, dated March 28th, 1890 (D. B. vol. 693, page 274), the heirs also taking title as devisees under the will of Henrietta W. Osburn dated October 3rd, 1899 (Will Book 97, page 234). The Osburn heirs on July 30th, 1924, conveyed to the School District of the

Borough of Sewickley for $30,000.00 (D. B. vol. 2224, page 365) and on August 8th, 1924, Louise W. Wilson, a daughter of Henrietta W. Osburn, conveyed to the same for $5,000.00 the "Reisinger lot" at the corner of Graham and Bank Streets, fronting 87.75 feet on Bank by 117.3 feet in depth, which had been sold to her by the other Osburn heirs February 7th, 1896 (D. B. vol. 922, page 459).

Mrs. Gilmore died April 18th, 1920, and by her will (Will Book 162, page 420) she left her residence with the acreage surrounding it to her grandchildren, Edward G. Cunningham and Harriet C. Orth, who on July 1st, 1924 (D. B. vol. 2238, page 206), sold it to the School District of the Borough of Sewickley for $28,000.00 (excepting a portion conveyed by them October 17th, 1923, to Martha Williams. D. B. vol. 2170, page 354).

Thus the title to both the Warner and Osburn properties was vested in the Sewickley School Board, and after the razing of the two homesteads, the High School building and athletic field were located on the line dividing *Aleppo* and *Loretto*.

PITTSBURGH IN 1815

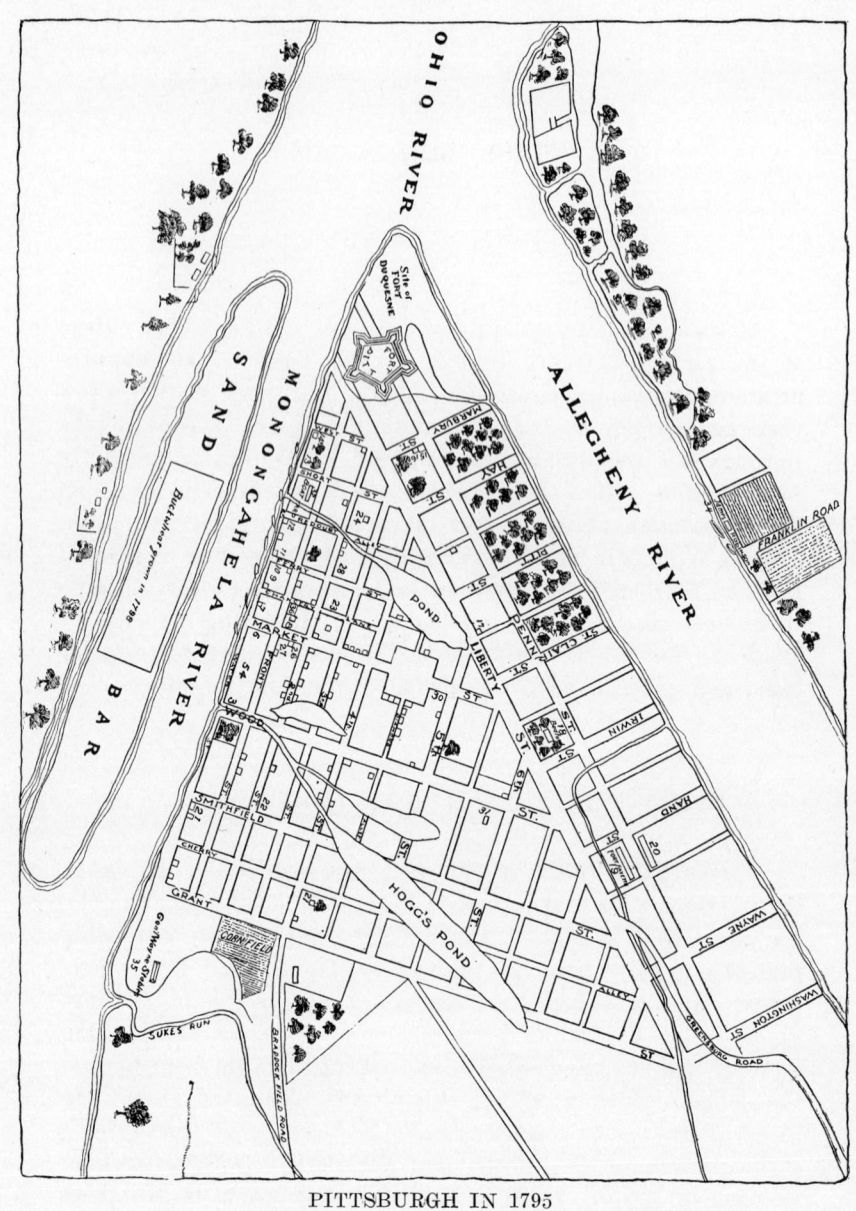

PITTSBURGH IN 1795
From *Life and Reminiscences*, by Wm. G. Johnston
By permission

PITTSBURGH IN 1815

BY WAY OF APPENDIX

As some of the foregoing papers relate to a Sewickley village of the early nineteenth century it was deemed not inappropriate to publish in connection with these a paper written a few years ago, though not for publication, giving some account of the Borough of Pittsburgh as it was in 1815, Pittsburgh being rightly considered as within the metropolitan district of Sewickley. In the preparation of that paper much material was drawn from Charles W. Dahlinger's *Pittsburgh: A Sketch of its Early Social Life*, an extremely entertaining and informative book of more than local interest. In publishing the following paper, Mr. Dahlinger's consent was given to the use of excerpts from his book, and grateful acknowledgment is due him therefor.

F. T. N.

* * *

Pittsburgh in the year 1815 was still a borough. It was in the following year that it became a city—obtained a city charter. Its population numbered about 9,000, thus slightly exceeding that of our three boroughs, Sewickley, Osborn and Edgeworth, today. Just a village, but already it had begun to disprove the assertion of Arthur Lee, who, as a visitor in 1784, taking note of the squalor, the hogs rooting in the streets and the sullen demeanor of the inhabitants, predicted that "the place will never be considerable." No account of Pittsburgh's early days and its growth and prosperity fails to include mention of Arthur Lee's unfavorable description of the place and of the people, "almost entirely Scots and Irish who live in paltry loghouses and are as dirty as in the North of Ireland, or even Scotland." Mr. Lee to the contrary notwithstanding, there were, even in 1784, decent and respectable Pittsburghers to whom his words did not apply. Perhaps he got in with the wrong set.

Mr. John Melish, an English traveler, was favorably impressed with Pittsburgh when he visited it in 1811. He predicted that it would "in all probability become one of the largest towns in America." He goes on to say: "With the spirit of enterprise which is exhibited in Pittsburgh I have no hesitation in hazarding an opinion that it will become one of the greatest manufacturing towns in the world. Besides the supply of the town and country round with manufactures it has a vast export trade, principally down the Ohio. The various manufactures in Pittsburgh exceed a million of dollars annually and we may calculate its progress in wealth from this data. A million of dollars is above $200.00 a year to every man, woman and child in Pittsburgh; or taking them by families of five, it is $1,000.00 to a family, and the expenditure of a family does not, on an average, exceed one-third of that sum."

By 1815 the little town was well on its way to refute Mr. Lee. In that year the first Pittsburgh Directory was compiled and put forth by Mr. James M. Riddle, its title page announcing an "Appendix Containing a Variety of Useful Information." The information is certainly *various,* though some of it has lost its *usefulness*—as for instance—the "Rules for Reducing the Currencies of the Different States into each other"—and "for Reducing the Currencies of the States to Dollars"; the "Method of Procedure in Obtaining Bounties," etc. Mr. Riddle gives the total population in that year as 9,431. Seven cities exceeded Pittsburgh in size. One notes with some surprise that after Philadelphia, New York, Baltimore and Boston, in that order, there follow Salem, Providence and Richmond. Then came Pittsburgh, as number eight.

Already the town was becoming a manufacturing center— as I shall note more particularly later on. An impressive list of manufactories ends with mention of "three large breweries, two white lead factories, three large rope-walks and two white and three green glass houses where the amount of glass annually manufactured is estimated at $200,000.00, and where glass cutting is also executed equal to any in Europe." There! That for you, Mr. Arthur Lee!

In order to visualize the scene of action, the stage on which the pioneer drama of Pittsburgh is unfolded, a brief glance at the physical setting is necessary—a look at the city map as it appeared in 1815. First of all you will note the extremely modest extent of the settlement. Clinging for the most part to the banks of the two rivers, it spread somewhat more sparsely toward the east as far as Grant's Hill. The general plan of the streets remains the same today; only the names have in many cases have been changed. All of the Avenues running parallel with the Monongahela—First to Seventh—were then called Streets, and First was then known as Front Street. Diamond Alley was just replacing the name Hammond Alley, and we ourselves recollect when Oliver Avenue was Virgin Alley (the Allée of the Assumption of the Blessed Virgin, as the builders of Fort Duquesne named it). A little thoroughfare called King Alley ran between Virgin Alley and Fifth Street. Penn and Liberty, paralleling the Allegheny river, have retained their original names, but the streets crossing them have not. In 1815 these cross streets were called (beginning at the Point) Water Street, Marbury, Pitt, Cecil's Alley, St. Clair (now Federal), Irwin, Irwin's Alley, Hand and Wayne (now Tenth Streets.

The streets running down to the Monongahela were West and Short Streets, Redoubt Alley, Ferry Street, Chancery Lane (also called Jail Alley), Market, Wood and Smithfield Streets, (the latter named for Devereux Smith, whose farm it crossed). Cherry Alley, Grant and Ross Streets. That takes us to the outermost limits of the town.

Speaking of Jail Alley—the Directory locates a number of estimable citizens between Jail Alley and Liberty!—a somewhat tantalizing situation, it would seem. More precarious even was that of one William Bennett—viz, on Liberty but "at the mouth of Jail alley."

So much then for the general plan and outline of the borough. It occupied that restricted district now the heart of downtown Pittsburgh, called by present day realtors "The Golden Triangle." The two rivers bounded it on north and south, no bridges as yet spanning them, while to the east rose Grant's Hill, named as you all know for Major Grant of the British army who met defeat there in 1758 at the hands of the French and Indians. Grant's Hill was a real barrier. No thoroughfare led up its precipitous face, other than certain goat paths by whose devious course the summit was reached, though the more gentle approach from the Monongahela river, or from the direction of Liberty street was usually employed. It is hard for us to realize this today, for Grant's Hill has not only been physically reduced since that day, but even in name it has come down to be called by us "The Hump." Three times has its top been shaved off. In 1836 the cut was ten feet, at Grant street and Fifth avenue, with a fill of four feet at Smithfield. In 1848 seven feet more were taken off and two feet filled in below. And finally, in 1912, the Hump was lowered fourteen feet, thus reducing the height of the hill by a total of thirty-seven feet. So you see, originally it was quite an eminence.

Once arrived at the summit, one was repaid by the extensive view over town and forest, with glimpses of the rivers in the distance. Grant's Hill was a favorite pleasure ground for the townspeople and charming descriptions may be read of its pleasant walks and wooded picnic grounds. Here was located Marie's Tavern, the favorite resort for parties of pleasure, famous in a town of many taverns for the hospitality of its proprietor, a genial Frenchman. Overlooking the town it stood, amidst gravelled walks and cultivated grounds in the center of a six acre tract where now stand the Court House and the City-County building.

Not yet had the smoke risen in such volume as to obscure the view. Fogs? Yes, they had fogs, but how different from the fogs of the present day! The first number of the *Gazette* contains a graphic description of Pittsburgh's surroundings and climate, and while it is dated some years earlier than the period assigned to this paper, yet doubtless the description fits the conditions as they were in the year 1815—(if it fits at all!).

"It may be observed," says the writer, "that at the junction of these two rivers until 8:00 o'clock of summer mornings a light fog is usually incumbent, but it is of a salutary nature, inasmuch as it consists of vapour not exhaled from stagnant water, but which the sun of the preceding day had extracted from trees and flowers, and in the evening had sent back in dew, so that rising with a second sun in fog, and becoming of aromatic quality, it is experienced to be healthful." "I was greatly struck," the writer continues, "in a summer morning, viewing from the ground the early vapour rising from the river. It hung midway between the foot and summit of the hill, so that the green above had the appearance of an island in the clouds." Reading this, one can only murmur "Alas!"

Mention has been made of the fill at Fifth and Smithfield in connection with the cutting down of Grant's Hill. This was a necessary measure owing to the presence there of quite a considerable body of water euphoniously called Hogg's Pond. Early maps show this pond extending diagonally from a point near the present ramp of the Pennsylvania railroad station to Fourth avenue, west of Smithfield, where it narrowed to a stream which emptied into the Monongahela at Wood street. Another somewhat smaller pond lay between Hogg's Pond and Wood street and a third one, still smaller, west of Wood and between Second and Fourth avenues. There was still another pond, and quite a large one, along Liberty at about Ferry street which emptied into the Monongahela below Redoubt alley. The river bank was high and steep and the only access to the beach was by way of the two ravines, one at Wood street, the other below Ferry, where these two small watercourses ran.

Here we will end our topography lesson and consider Pittsburgh in its business and social aspects; not exhaustively, of course, but necessarily in a very sketchy manner.

Pittsburgh was a town built by pioneers, a settlement carved out of the primeval forest. In this it was no different from other pioneer communities. What made it different was the rugged character of its Scotch-Irish founders on the one hand and, on the other, its situation at what was a strategic point, for it lay at the very gateway to the great illimitable West. As soon as the roads were built over the mountains in the East, the pioneers came by hundreds, then by thousands, seeking new homes in the Mississippi Valley.

Being at the gateway it was necessarily the re-shipping point where goods brought over the mountains by wagons were unpacked and loaded again on boats destined for points west by way of the Ohio River. Thus the settlement at the head of navigation became the outfitting place for the western voyagers. This encouraged manufactures. Here was the market for all sorts of goods. Here, too, were the natural resources which supplied the raw materials and here were the industrious and skillful artisans, themselves pioneers, schooled in self-reliance and inventive ingenuity, who set themselves to the task of supplying what the settlers needed. Pots and spinning wheels these home makers required. Axes, horseshoes, candle molds, flails, guns, cow bells—every sort of thing almost, the villagers learned to make to supply the trade.

By 1815, the Directory tells us, the town boasted of a steam engine factory, three air foundries—by which is not meant "free air and crank case service," but places "where castings of every description from a cannon to a spider are extensively and handsomely executed"; an anvil and anchor factory, a brass foundry, a butt hinge factory, a pattern maker's shop with steam lathes, a wire factory, a steam flour mill, rolling mill, paper mill, a cotton factory, and the breweries and glass factories mentioned above. A stirring little community it was, already beginning, with its foundries and steam engine factories, to be noted for its most famous product—smoke. To these industries were added saw-mills, tan-yards, lime kilns and boat building docks where "The Mississippi Steamboat Company" built boats "on Fulton's plan" to transport the emigrants and their outfits to their promised land.

A surprising diversity of employment appears from a glance at the first Directory. Beside the usual vocations such as carpenter, saddler, brewer, merchant, cooper, turner, glassmaker, etc., we note many that are strange to us and unusual today. Such as hair cap maker, card maker (these cards were not to be played with; they were combs used in carding wool and hemp), bow-string maker, blue dyer, reed maker, ship joiner, glover, hot nailor, bridle bit and sword maker, makers of candlesticks, snuffers, chimney-hooks, horse fleams, wallowers for Dutch fans, boulting cloth makers and many others. I note one maker of piano fortes—also a Windsor chair maker.

By this time the benighted Scotch-Irish of Arthur Lee's day had been joined by considerable numbers of English and German settlers; although the Directory lists no less than 109 names beginning with "Mac" or "Mc." In 1815, we are told that the buildings of a public character were "a handsome octagon Episcopal church, a handsome and spacious Presbyterian church, also a Covenanters', a German Lutheran, and a Roman Catholic church, and an Academy, all of brick; a courthouse, jail, three incorporated banks, a dramatic theatre, a Masonic hall, three market houses, one in the Diamond and two in Second street, and several mercantile and financial building of a substantial character."

They had long ceased to lack places of worship. The Protestant Episcopal at the junction of Wood and Liberty streets; the First Presbyterian on Wood street where McCreery's store now stands; the Second Presbyterian on the northwestern corner of Diamond alley and Smithfield street (now Frank & Seder's store); a Roman Catholic chapel at the upper end of Liberty; the Seceders on the north side of Seventh street (now Seventh avenue) east of Liberty; the Covenanters, close by; the Methodists on the north side of Front street (now First avenue) between Wood and Smithfield, and the German Lutheran on land granted by the Penns, east side of Smithfield above Fifth, where it stands today, generously sharing its site with Woolworth's 5 & 10c store.

With the sparsely settled shores to the north and south there was communication only by ferry. No bridges spanned the two rivers then, as I have said. The oldest ferry, known as Jones's, crossed the Monongahela at the Point. The boats were propelled by horse power. Another, Henderson's, was located farther up Water street and a third, still farther up, called Gregg's, or The Upper Ferry. Each ferryman conducted a tavern as a side line. To cross the Allegheny, one patronized James Robinson's ferry which connected with Franklin Road— now Federal street. Apparently as an inducement to prospective settlers, he advertised, "All persons going to and returning from sermon, and all funerals, free ferriage."

While we are free to assume that the burghers were diligent in attending divine worship, there is no need to assume anything with regard to the popularity of the taverns. There is ample testimony to this fact. Considering the size of the community there was a multitude of inns. As early as 1808 they numbered twenty-four. The constant flow of west-bound travel assured abundant support, and in addition to the transient trade there was the regular patronage by all classes of the townspeople. Tavern keeping and liquor selling were of such respectability that many of the most esteemed citizens were, or had been, tavern-keepers or had sold liquors, or distilled whisky, or brewed beer. Elders of church, choir leaders, precentors, deacons, thought it no disgrace to engage in the business.

The taverns, scattered here and there throughout the town, clustered most thickly along Market street and that vicinity. They were known by names displayed on signs hung over the sidewalks, as—"The Sign of General Washington," "The Sign of General Butler," "The Sign of the Crossed Keys," "The Sign of the Green Tree," "The Sign of the Waggon," "The Sign of the Whale and the Monkey," etc.

Semple's Tavern, at the corner of Water and Ferry streets, was one of the oldest and best. Here George Washington stayed in 1770,—and it was only in the year 1909 that it was torn down. How many of us ever saw it? John Marie's inn on Grant's Hill I have already mentioned. It partook, more or less, of the character of an out-of-town roadhouse, though one of great respectability.

Downtown, the taverns supplied the demand for places of public assembly, for the holding of political conferences, as Masonic lodge rooms, etc. Certain political cliques regularly foregathered at certain taverns, while their rivals met and orated at other inns near by. Orating and whisky drinking flourished to an enormous extent. The taste for these two luxuries seems to have been universal and insatiable. Perhaps one was cause and the other effect; at all events they went hand in hand. No moral stigma attached to the consumption of whisky. How they got away with it in such quantities is a marvel today. Judge Veech in writing of these times declares that whisky "was the indispensable emblem of hospitality and the accompaniment of labor in every pursuit, the stimulant in joy and the solace in grief. It was the omnipresent beverage of old and young, men and women, and he was a churl who stinted it." The farmer placed a jug under a tree beside the hayfield for the refreshment of the mowers; the merchant sealed his bargain with his customer in a friendly glass. The lawyer— but the less said, the better. "Even the minister," says Judge Veech, "partook of it before going to church, and after he came back," and frequently was known to keep a brown bottle under his reading desk from which he would take a pull before launching into his discourse. Charles Dahlinger in his book, *Pittsburgh: A Sketch of its Early Social Life,* tells of a practical joke perpetrated by the Rev. John McMillan on the Rev. Joseph Patterson, another of the early ministers in this region which illustrates the custom of drinking among the clergy.

On their way to attend a meeting of the Synod, the two ministers stopped at a wayside inn and called for whisky, which was set before them. Mr. Patterson asked a blessing which was rather lengthy. Dr. McMillan meanwhile drank the whisky, and to Mr. Patterson's blank look remarked blandly, "You should watch as well as pray." Dr. McMillan was a leader in the movement for education. He founded Canonsburg Academy which later became Jefferson College.

Market street was the civic center. On it were located the chief taverns and the principal stores, where the merchant usually lived on the second floor above his place of business. From Front street to the Diamond the stores and residences were now continuous, with no vacant lots between. Here were gathered the élite of the town, social and professional. Here were published the rival newspapers, John Scull's *Pittsburgh Gazette*, Brackenridge's *Tree of Liberty*, of opposite political faith, and, later, *The Commonwealth*.

On Market, at its junction with the Diamond, had been erected in 1789 the "new courthouse," a substantial two-story brick building with hip roof and bell tower, facing east on the square. It served its purpose till 1841, when the first court house on Grant's Hill was built. Facing the court house to the east stood a semi-circular market house with wide projecting roof supported by brick pillars where the country people displayed their produce for sale, while within were stalls where butchers sold their meats.

On the west side of Market street, between Front and Second streets, lived Zadok Kramer, over his book shop and printing establishment, at the sign of the Franklin Head. Benjamin Franklin was the patron saint of everyone who had any connection, however remote, with printing. Here were supplied reading matter and such novels as were rather meagerly put forth in that day. Here Kramer published his *Navigator* which furnished valuable information to intending western travelers and which went through several annual editions. Kramer's bookshop was the headquarters of the intelligentsia. His influence as writer and publisher was a beneficent one and did not fade out at his death.

Physicians and lawyers had their homes and offices on Market street—which, by the way, prior to the building of the new court house and market on the Diamond, was known as "Main street." Gradually the trend of building was toward the Diamond and Fifth street. The east side of Market, between Third and Fourth, was especially important as the residence section and headquarters of a powerful political junta or ring known as Clapboard Row. Sort of a local Tammany Hall it was, from whence went forth open propaganda and secret instructions looking to the political domination of the town. "Clapboard Row" was the object of vitriolic attacks in the columns of the newspaper of opposite faith. *Vitriolic* is the word. No newspaper today would venture to indulge in such personal abuse as was usual in those days. Duels sometimes followed—though duelling was forbidden by statute. One particularly sad affair was that of Tarleton Bates, a handsome young Southerner, who was challenged by one Ephraim Pentland as the result of a libellous article that appeared in the *Tree of Liberty*. Bates horsewhipped Pentland in public and the challenge followed. The duel took place next day in a ravine in Oakland, near the Monongahela river at a point now occupied by the lower end of Jones & Laughlin's ore yard. Bates was killed. The event is commemorated today by a street named for him, which runs down through the length of that ravine.

While on the subject of newspapers, it might not be uninteresting to quote an advertisement culled here and there from the current issues. Slavery had existed to a limited extent up to a few years prior to 1815. The Act of Assembly of March, 1780, provided that all negroes and mulattoes born after that date, of slave mothers, should become free upon arriving at the age of twenty-eight years. Advertisements offering slaves for sale no longer appeared in the papers, but a few years earlier the following was not an unusual notice:

> "FOR SALE: A Black woman, who has six years and a half to serve, with two female children, from four to six years of age, to serve till twenty-eight. The woman is healthy, honest and industrious and an excellent cook. The owner having no further occasion for their services will dispose of them on moderate terms. Enquire at the *Gazette* office."

Or the following:

> "FOR SALE: A Black girl who has eleven years and eight months to serve. She is young, active and healthy; a good

house-maid and equally qualified for farm or tavern work."

The apprentice system was in vogue. There appears to have been no such anxiety for the recovery of a runaway apprentice as attended the escape of a slave, rewards of $20, $30 and $50 being offered for the latter. Here is the proof:

"Five Cents Reward is offered for the return of a runaway apprentice in the tin plate business. The above reward will be paid if brought home, but no expenses."

Or again:

"Three cents and a pound of old horseshoe nails reward for the return of a strayed blacksmith's apprentice. The above reward, no charges and no thanks, will be given to any person who will return said stray."

An explanation of these perfunctory advertisements lies probably in the fact that the Act of April 11, 1799, relating to absconding apprentices, placed upon the runaway, when he should reach the age of twenty-one years, liability in an action at law, which is not defined in the Act, but which was presumably an action to recover for support and maintenance furnished by the master. The apprenticeship agreement called for nurture and instruction by the master or mistress and, on the part of the apprentice, for service; and when these obligations ceased to be mutual, the parties were released. Hence the necessity for public notice of the apprentice's flight, even though the master should be indifferent as to his return.

Time is lacking even to skim through the advertisements, many of which are quaint, amusing and sometimes incongruous in content and make-up. As where a gentleman advertises the flight of his wife, Fanny, from his bed and board, which compels him, though reluctantly (he says) to forbid all persons to trust her on his account; then goes on to say that he begs to inform those who wish to be shaved in Imperial style that he is always to be found at his shop in Market street between Front and Water streets.

Here is one headed—in capitals—"OYSTERS" "John Byrne at his Umbrella Manufactory, 4th between Market and Ferry streets. Just received and for sale at his Oyster House a few kegs of most excellent Spiced Oysters. He continues to make and repair Umbrellas, and Parasols in the newest manner; the smallest favour will be gratefully attended to." Again, under the caption "OYSTERS," "Gentlemen can be genteely accommodated at the City Hall with Oysters."

Here is one with an old-time flavor: "John Cowan announces that he has removed his Bow String Manufactory from Liberty street to the house lately occupied by William Davis, Sign of the Bird in Hand."

Many of the advertisements reflect the social life of the day. Evidently the strictest of the Scotch-Irish were losing their grip a little, for there begin to appear occasional advertisements of dancing instructors, music masters—and even of public balls! This one gives, it would seem, cruelly short notice of the event: "M. Boudet respectfully informs the Ladies and Gentlemen of Pittsburgh and its vicinity that he will give a Ball this evening—(Friday the 24th inst.) at the Court House at half past seven o'clock, and will be conducted as they are in populous cities, viz: the ladies to be invited, and gentlemen to pay one dollar on their admission—understood that such gentlemen as are strangers to the professor must come introduced by some person with whom he is acquainted, without which they cannot be admitted. N. B. No gentleman allowed to dance in boots. Tickets to be had at the door. Price one dollar."

If the dance, then why not the theatre? So thought some of the wild younger element, to the scandalizing of the older generation. Private theatricals formed the entering wedge. Two dramatic societies existed as early as 1808 and a third was organized in 1812. But this godless form of entertainment met with little encouragement, in fact with much opposition. Even stronger was the feeling against the professional play actors who now and then came to town. Gradually the bolder and more broad-minded citizens learned to frequent the play house, but it would seem that even they felt constrained, as not knowing quite when to applaud, perhaps lacking the self confidence to express such emotions as the play aroused. The editor of the *Commonwealth,* in an issue at about this time, complains of the coldness of Pittsburgh's reception of visiting artists: "The Theatre of this City has been now opened nearly a fortnight," he writes, "and the managers, although they have used every exertion to please, in the selection of their pieces, have not been enabled to pay the contingent expenses of the House. This is a severe satire on the taste of this place." "It is to be hoped that the correct and manly acting of Mr. Savage and the chastened elegance which Mrs. Savage is said to exhibit, will attract to the Theatre for this one evening at least the friends to this rational amusement." Once lured into the naughty precincts, it would seem that the audience felt ill at ease.

On one occasion Hamlet was the offering, the title role taken by one Hutton, an actor from the East. In modern parlance the play was a flop. The manager, a Mr. Entwisle, determined to reach his audience, put on a raw burlesque of Hamlet the following night, himself taking the leading part and making it a broad farce. A traveler from the sophisticated East—let us hope he exaggerated somewhat—wrote of the performance: "The audience were solemn, serious and dull. The affecting entrance of the deranged Ophelia, who, instead of rosemary, rue, etc., carried an ample supply of turnips and carrots, did not cause them to move a muscle of their intelligent faces, the ladies, indeed, excepted, who evinced by the frequent use of their pocket handkerchiefs that their sympathies were engaged on the side of the love-sick maiden—." The writer goes on to say that a respectable lawyer assured him next morning that he had been at the play, "And sir," he said, "I do not think that Mr. Entwisle acted Hamlet quite so well as Mr. Hutton." Let us hope that the story is merely an early example of the kind of gibes at Pittsburgh's expense which are not unknown today.

Howbeit, if the theatre was an unaccustomed pleasure to which the people generally were untrained, no restraint hedged them about in their enjoyment of the horse races. Unbounded hilarity prevailed. The race course was located on the outskirts to the northeast of the town between Liberty Street and the Allegheny River. The races were conducted under the auspices of the Jockey Club, which had been in existence for many years.

(I am quoting now from Mr. Dahlinger's book.) "Sportsmen came from all the surrounding country. The races were under the saddle, for sulkies had not been invented. Racing proprieties were observed and jockeys were required to be dressed in jockey habits." Quoting another historian—"The races were an affair of all-engrossing interest. The whole town was daily poured forth to witness them. Schools and shops were shut up or deserted. This was an annual event, in the autumn, and lasted three days. The plain within the course and near it was filled with booths as at a fair, where everything was said and done and sold and eaten or drunk, where frequent fights occurred, dogs barked and bit, horses trod on men's toes and booths fell down on people's heads." Truly a good time was had by all, though there were not lacking voices that were raised in protest against the riot and license and particularly against the gambling that accompanied the sport.

Another popular form of entertainment was furnished by the militia companies, at their semi-annual exhibitions and drills. The fact that the rival companies represented differing shades of political opinion added to the zest of the occasion. The Revolution and the Indian fighting had left a decided military stamp on the people and, in what day or generation has not the glamour of gold lace, cockades and waving plumes had a strong hold on the popular imagination?

The parade ground was the level part of Grant's Hill which adjoined Marie's tavern on the northeast. Here twice a year the militia received its training, furnishing unbounded enjoyment and patriotic thrills for the multitude.

It is easy to lay too much emphasis upon the dour and cold religious nature of the Scotch-Irish, and to lose sight of the fact that there was life and gayety in the town. Perhaps the unco' guid did not partake of it, but there were many, less strait-laced, who did. Charming pictures are drawn by some of the early writers of the comforts and luxuries of the homes, of the pleasant winter evenings spent in the blaze of generous open fires or around the more economical Franklin stoves, where games of cards—chiefly "whisk" (as it was called) and "Boston"—were enjoyed and the young ones made merry with song and even dancing, while without, the night watchman on his rounds called the hours and notified all intending robbers of his approach. One old German watchman had a well-known cry, "Past 2 o'glock; cold vedder and de moon peeps out vunce or dwice."

Small affairs were given in the homes; the large ones, called "Assemblies," usually in the new court house or in the taverns which had rooms set apart for dances. The Sign of the Green Tree had an "Assembly Room"; The Sign of General Butler and The Sign of the Waggon each had a "Ball Room." There were also concerts which may not have measured up to the modern Harvey Gaul standard, but which were enjoyed none the less.

The stately and picturesque costumes of Colonial days had passed. The influence of the French Revolution is shown in the more sober dress of both women and men. Here and there an old-timer still clung to the ruffles, knee breeches and queues of an earlier day, but for the most part the men wore tight-fitting full-length trousers in rather neutral colors, with coats and waistcoats of more lively shades. Stocks with high colors upheld the chin, while the head was covered and adorned with a tall hat of beaver, castor or roram. Castor was made of silk in imitation of beaver, while roram was made of felt with a beaver facing. These were for the town folk. The country people were more simply clothed, in homespun or linsey woolsey. The men wore short, round reefer-like coats, wide long trousers and squarish black felt hats, while from the remoter settlements appeared smock-like garments died in walnut juice, with here and there the tanned deer-skin still popular in the backwoods. Mr. Dahlinger, after enumerating a great variety of materials and dress goods obtainable in the shops of that day says: "Other articles were tamboured petticoats, tamboured cravats, silk and cotton shawls, wreaths and plumes, sunshades and parasols, black silk netting gloves, white and salmon colored long and short gloves, kid and morocco shoes and slippers, men's beaver, tanned and silk gloves, men's cotton and thread caps and silk and cotton hose.''

While we occasionally indulge in a smile at the quaintness of the people of a hundred years ago, the crudeness of their amusements, the simplicity of their mode of life, and are prone to patronize them as we look back smugly from the height of our modern civilization, let us not lose sight of the fact that they were sturdy pioneers, far-seeing men, conquerors of the wilderness, builders of the foundations of our industrial supremacy. They accomplished a task which we, softened by our life amid such creature comforts as they never imagined, could not begin to do. They were not all cold and narrow religionists as some would have us believe. They were not all boors. Many a cultured gentleman there was in those days, many a sweet and gracious hostess, dispensing cheer and hospitality in tasteful and well furnished homes.

Some accounts of those days to be sure, leaning to the biographical and the genealogical, perhaps overemphasize this social side of the picture. An impartial historian should show both sides—the cultivated and courtly gentleman of the old school, and on the other hand the roystering turbulent frequenter of the wayside tavern, with the quiet industrial artisan and home builder occupying the middle of the picture. In the words of Mr. Dahlinger, ''All that Pittsburgh has been and much that it is destined to be can be traced to the ground-work laid by those early leaders. The history and progress of the place is a continual reminder of their shrewdness and foresight. Pittsburgh has always gone forward in culture and refinement, no less than in wealth. The greatest iron and steel center in the world is the monument of those pioneers. All honor to them!''

March 14th, 1927.

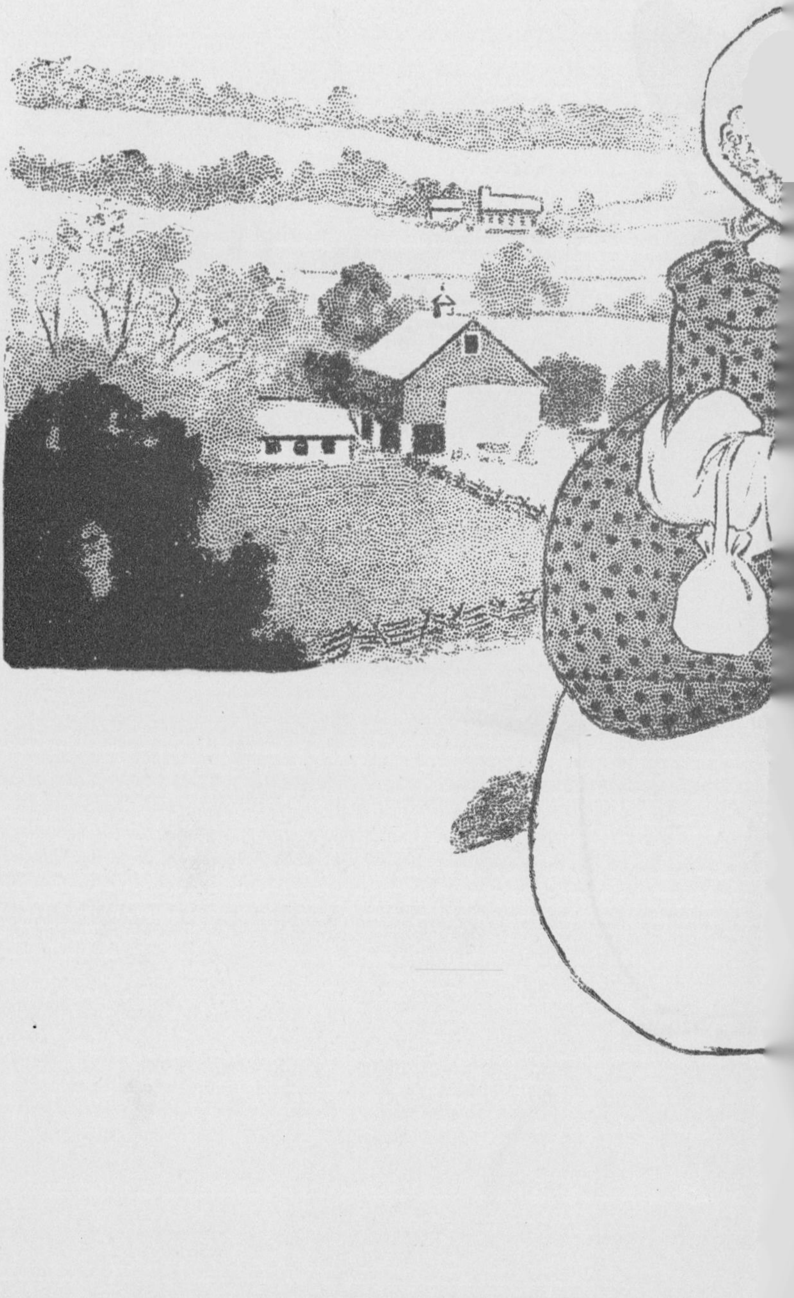